The Gospel of St. Mark

The Gospel of St. Mark

A Cycle of Ten Lectures

Rudolf Steiner

Anthroposophic Press
Bell's Pond, Hudson, New York

Rudolf Steiner Press
London

The ten lectures presented here were given in Basel, Switzerland from the 15th to the 24th of September, 1912. In the Collected Edition of Rudolf Steiner's works, the volume containing the German texts is entitled *Das Markus-Evangelium* (Vol. 139 in the Bibliographic Survey, 1961). They were translated from the German by Conrad Mainzer and edited by Stewart C. Easton.

Distributed in the United States by Anthroposophic Press, Star Route, Hudson, New York 12534
Distributed in the United Kingdom by Rudolf Steiner Press, 38 Museum St., London WC 1

Library of Congress Cataloging-in-Publication Data

Steiner, Rudolf, 1861–1925.
    The Gospel of St. Mark.

    "The ten lectures . . . were given in Basel,
Switzerland from the 15th to the 24th of September,
1912. In the Collected edition of Rudolf Steiner's
works, the volume containing the German texts is
entitled Das Markus-Evangelium (vol. 139 in the
Bibliographic survey, 1961)"—T.p. verso.
    1. Bible. N.T. Mark—Criticism, interpretation,
etc.—Addresses, essays, lectures. I. Easton,
Stewart Copinger, 1907-   . II. Title.
III. Title: Gospel of St. Mark.
BS2585.S7713   1986   226'.306   86-1215
ISBN 0-88010-082-6
        0-88010-083-4 (pbk.)

Cover motif from sketch by Rudolf Steiner for *Anthroposophie, Österreichischer Bote von Menschengeist zu Menschengeist,* 1922.

Printed in the United States of America

Contents and Synopsis

Different perspectives of history in nineteenth century
by comparison with earlier centuries. Sudden entry of
Oriental literature into Western culture in nineteenth
century. General cultural intermingling, Oriental
interest in Christianity. New interest in questions that
can be answered only out of spiritual science. Opening
words of Mark Gospel, how they can be understood.
Difference between period before and period after
Mystery of Golgotha. Hector and Empedocles of pre-
Christian times; Hamlet and Faust of Christian era.
How earlier personalities find difficulty in adjusting to
life in Christian era. Why such a contrast? Mystery of
Golgotha and coming of the Christ between these incarnations. Gospels as revelations from world of hierarchies to world of earth, reaching man through medium
of angeloi. The ev-angel or Gospel.

Need to study Bible rightly and to perceive especially
its artistic composition. Culmination of Old Testament
in books of Maccabees and martyrdom of seven sons of
widow. Mingling of Persian and Hebrew element in
Zarathustra Jesus-child. Hebrew prophets as former
initiates of other peoples; receivers of inspiration, not

v

initiates in Hebrew incarnation. Development of consciousness during course of Old Testament history. Coming of Christ as fulfillment of Old Testament prophesy. John the Baptist as divine messenger, last of old prophets, forerunner of Christ. Recognition of John by Jews, recognition of Christ by supersensible beings. Twelve apostles as reincarnated sons of Mattathias and sons of the widow. Judas Iscariot as Judas Maccabaeus and in unnamed later incarnation. Human evolution as work of art. Christianity as world religion, free from nationalism.

John the Baptist as reincarnated Elijah whose earthly manifestation was Naboth. Elijah as folk-soul of Hebrew people. Baptism by John, its relation to task of Elijah and as preparation for coming of Christ. Continued activity of spirit of Elijah-John after his physical death. Christ among disciples of John. John's later incarnation as Raphael. Hermann Grimm's inability to write biography of Raphael. Increase of bread through Elijah and Christ's "miracle" of loaves and fishes. Contrast between complete incarnation of Christ and incomplete incarnation of Elijah in Naboth. Healings by Christ Jesus, nature of so-called "miracles." Contrast with healings by physicians trained in Mystery schools. Healings and karma, "forgiveness of sins." Bible as book for all mankind, not only Christians. How Buddhists and Christians should recognize each other's religions.

The mission of Gautama Buddha and his inspired teaching in India. The work of Socrates in Greece and its influence in the West. Its appeal to reasoning power of his pupils. Contrast between Buddha and Socrates. Socrates occasionally close to Buddha (e.g. in *Phaedo*); Buddha occasionally close to Socrates. Christ Jesus among his disciples. Example of Parable of the Sower. Difference in his way of speaking to disciples and to the crowd, with its heritage of ancient clairvoyance. Sentient soul heritage in Buddha, consciousness soul anticipation in Socrates, two diverging "comets," both living in age of mind soul.

five thousand and the four thousand. Intermingling of earthly and spiritual in Mark Gospel. Peter's acknowledgment of Christ and its sequel. World historical monologue of Christ Jesus.

Relation between Christ Jesus and the Twelve. Contrast between initiates of other peoples and Hebrew prophets. Disciples' ignorance of initiation, hence difficulty of understanding Mystery of Golgotha. Before Mystery of Golgotha spiritual worlds unable to penetrate into human "I"; hence the "I" could enter spiritual worlds only in initiation when outside body—spiritual ego-force then too strong for physical body, able to enter only damaged or vulnerable bodies, e.g. Achilles' heel, Siegfried and Oedipus. The five wounds of Christ. As result of Mystery of Golgotha possibility now exists to perceive it in imagination and to understand it. This understanding particularly necessary for disciples. Contrast between Yoga and Oriental philosophy, attained through clairvoyance, and Western philosophy. Beginnings of Western philosophy. Pherecydes of Syros as last straggler from clairvoyant period. Thales and other pre-Socratics as transition from clairvoyance to nonclairvoyant thinking and abstract concepts. Empedocles as transitional figure—his "call" answered by a "cry" from Golgotha.

Occult significance of mountain, lake and plain. Transfiguration on mountain. Moses as bearer of initiation streams of other peoples. Hebrew people as gift of God to mankind. Sacrifice of Isaac. Phinehas, grandson of Aaron and his "zeal" for God. His later incarnation as Elijah-Naboth. Moses, Elijah, and Christ as cosmic deity, at Transfiguration. Presence of Peter, James and John at Transfiguration; their inability to understand it. Judas Iscariot and the woman with alabaster flask of ointment. Meaning of the "curse" of the fig tree, "no longer the time of figs." Bodhi tree of Buddha and the tree of the Cross.

Artistic composition of Mark Gospel, artistic threads that are also occult threads. Christ shown in this Gospel as cosmic being. Three possible levels of understanding of Mystery of Golgotha. Failure of disciples, of Jewish leaders, of Romans. Conversations with Sadducees and scribes regarding higher worlds not understood by disciples. Christ as "Son of David" not recognized by Jews. Pilate and Christ as "king of the Jews." Failure of chosen disciples to accompany Christ as far as Mystery of Golgotha. Recognition by Christ in Gethsemane of his own isolation. Recognition of Christ as Son of David only by blind Bartimaeus. Contrast between Christ working in world and Christ betrayed under cover of darkness. Gradual withdrawal of cosmic Christ from Jesus of Nazareth. Abandonment by the disciples, then by "the young man." Reappearance of "young man" after Resurrection. How could disciples who fled know truth about Mystery of Golgotha?

Change of attitude among Christians toward Gospels over the centuries. Influence of materialism. Jesus research and Christ research. Necessity of clairvoyance to understand Mystery of Golgotha. Transmission of clairvoyant knowledge from Peter to Mark. Mark's understanding of prospective decadence of humanity through experiences in Egypt. Recapitulation of Egyptian culture in our age. Materialistic science and spiritual science. Failure of humanity to recognize the Son of Man and impulse of cosmic Christ. Son of Man as highest ideal of humanity. How to experience this through Mark Gospel and its artistic composition. Difference in spiritual comprehension between men and women. Mary Magdalene at tomb. How Mystery of Golgotha will be understood and experienced in future. Difference between lives of Buddha and Christ. Unacceptable view of Christ held by official Theosophical Society. Only through impulse from Mystery of Golgotha can Mystery of Golgotha be understood. Primal Word enkindled through Christ. "Heaven and earth shall pass away but my words shall not pass away."

Introduction

In the non-anthroposophical world the Gospel of St. Mark is usually accorded relatively little attention. It is of course widely recognized as the earliest of the canonical Gospels, as it is also the shortest. Its historical importance is therefore not denied, especially as the source of much that is included in the more widely read Gospel of Matthew, the longest of the four. But its distinctive features are nowhere given as much importance as by Rudolf Steiner, who indeed devoted many lectures to various aspects of it (*Background to the Gospel of St. Mark*) before he embarked on the remarkable ten lectures given in Basel in September 1912 now being published in a third English edition. In the last of these lectures he tells us that he had now brought to a completion the program he had set himself many years earlier when he began his work on the Gospels with his many lectures in different cities on the ever popular Gospel of St. John. And this cycle was indeed to be the last he was to give on any of the four Gospels, the so-called Fifth Gospel of 1913 being of an entirely different nature.

From one point of view the Mark Gospel may be thought of as the most deeply esoteric of all, concerned as it was so exclusively with the cosmic Christ, Christ as a spiritual being who manifested Himself on earth through the body of Jesus of Nazareth, whereas John in his Gospel spoke of Him as the Divine Logos, the second person of the Trinity, a concept that presumably lay beyond the possibilities open to Mark through his particular initiation. Again in the last lecture of this cycle Steiner tells us how it happened that Mark came to perceive the Christ in His cosmic aspect. Mark, he tells us, was a pupil of Peter, who had come to his own understanding of the Christ through the inspiration of the Holy Spirit at the first Whitsuntide, which enabled him to perceive in clairvoyance the entire Mystery of Golgotha—although after his denial of Christ he had not been able to participate at all in the external events. Peter was able to awaken subsequently the same knowledge, the same *memory*, as Steiner calls it, of what he had not experienced, in his personal pupils, among whom was Mark. Mark then made his way to Alexandria in Egypt, where he was able to find "the outer environment that enabled him to give his Gospel the particular coloring it needed." In Alexandria he could absorb all that was to be found in the pagan gnosis, and he deeply experienced in his soul the corruption into which the world had fallen—exemplified, most particularly, in Egypt. It was this experience that led him to perceive so clearly the significance of the appearance of Christ Jesus on earth.

Almost nothing of the depths of the Mark Gospel can be grasped through an ordinary superficial reading of it, nor have biblical commentators, using their traditional methods within their traditional framework, been able to throw much light on it. For this Gospel, above all, someone like Rudolf Steiner was needed. Time and again Steiner draws attention to the wonderfully artistic composition of the Gospel, possible only to a Lion initiate like St. Mark. Especially in the last chapters of the Gospel, particularly the short twenty-verse conclusion in the final chapter that covers the whole period following the resurrection, every word counts, and nothing is left unsaid that from Mark's point of view was needed. Yet the usual view is that Mark was simply anxious to finish his book as expeditiously as possible since in describing the resurrection he had come to the end of what he wished to say. Fortunately, Steiner goes over the last chapter in great detail, and shows also how in the two previous chapters all manner of secrets were being revealed about Christ Himself and the future of mankind once the Christ Impulse had entered the world evolution. If we follow closely what Rudolf Steiner was trying to show to us, *how* to read this Gospel, it is impossible not to feel how each word, each episode, is carefully chosen by the evangelist to bring out the cosmic greatness of Christ, and at the same time the unspeakable suffering and loneliness of Him whom he calls the Son of Man, who is here, as nowhere else in Steiner's lectures, distinguished so clearly from the cosmic Christ-Being who dwelt for three years within the three sheaths of Jesus of Nazareth. It is only in the Mark Gospel that we are told of "the young man who fled away naked." This is the youthful Christ Impulse which thereafter reappears only once, in the form of the young man seen by Mary Magdalene and the other women at the sepulcher on Easter morning.

It goes without saying that no biblical commentator has ever been able to make sense of this "young man," who has even sometimes been identified by them as the writer of the Gospel himself. From what Steiner says it would seem that, of the four evangelists, only Mark perceived this being clairvoyantly and understood its significance, as it was Mark also who grasped the full poignancy of the scene in the Garden of Gethsemane when the disciples who had vowed to experience the Mystery of Golgotha with their Master could not remain awake, leaving Christ Jesus to undergo it alone. Immediately afterward in the Mark Gospel comes the betrayal and the flight of the disciples, following which the "young man," the Christ Impulse, also abandons Jesus of Nazareth, who as His last words from the Cross, as recorded by Mark and Matthew, was to utter the cry "My God, my God why has thou forsaken me?," words whose true meaning is here revealed in all its depth by Steiner. The cosmic Christ "hovered" over Jesus at the Crucifixion and surely experienced it, even though it was Jesus, the Son of Man, the highest ideal of man, as Steiner calls Him here, whom men should have revered as their highest ideal instead of spitting on Him and reviling Him, who was nailed to the Cross and died on it. Thus the divine being, the Christ, who could not as a divine being of His exalted rank actually die, could nevertheless experience death through the link He had forged with the three sheaths of Jesus during the three years since the Baptism, when He had lived in them as their "I."

This at least is the picture Steiner presents in this wonderful cycle, and not the least of the tasks he left to us is how we can reconcile what he said elsewhere about the necessity from a cosmic point of view for an immortal god to experience death as a man, with the very clear picture he presents here, a picture which, as he said, completed what he had undertaken to do when he first started to lecture on the Gospels. And we can never be sufficiently grateful for the fact that he was able to give this cycle before the disorders in the spiritual world that accompanied the first World War prevented him, as he was to reveal later, from ever giving any more cycles devoted entirely to one or the other of the Gospels.

Stewart C. Easton
Kinsale, Ireland
1985

Some Preliminary Remarks

Readers of this lecture-cycle who do not know from their own experience what was taking place when it was being delivered in the Theosophical Society, then headed by Annie Besant, will perhaps object to the polemical tone of several passages, especially those in which the conception of Christ held by this individuality is criticized. To understand this tone it must be realized that at that time the authority of Annie Besant still counted for much among many of those for whom the lectures were intended, and that the lecturer had to defend his own interpretation of Christ which, however, was in no way different from what he had hitherto maintained.

Now, since these battles lie far back in the past, some readers may well think that the polemical passages should be deleted. This is not the view of the present editors, who believe that, for historical reasons, the lectures should be preserved just as they were given. In addition, some readers may find it not without interest to know the superstitions against which the interpretation of Christ advanced here had to be defended, and how contrary to all Western feeling such superstitions were. Anyone who envisages the matter correctly is bound to see that for the lecturer it was really not a question of quarreling in the way characteristic of those societies and sects which hold their own views of the world. On the contrary what was at stake was the validity of his views, for which he had to answer before his own scientific conscience, as against a distorted belief motivated by personal interests. Reasonable people may certainly conclude that this belief was self-evidently absurd. Nevertheless it was such absurdities that were advanced in the Theosophical Society against what the lecturer had to say. In the world of reality, even things contrary to rational thinking may play their part.

Now, because the lecturer could not abandon his interpretation of Christ, which he had advanced since 1902 and which had been entirely unchallenged by leading members of the Theosophical Society, the Society, under Annie Besant's authority, among other similarly glorious deeds excluded all those members who, convinced by the lecturer's arguments, refused to accept Mrs. Besant's muddled beliefs. In this respect the Theosophical Society behaved like all inquisitors in a case which the lecturer himself had not thought of as a quarrel over dogma and had not treated as such. All he wished to do was to make an exposition based purely on facts. However, this is the kind of thing that usually happens when there is a collision between a valid factual presentation and a fanaticism reinforced by personal interests. In the course of time those who had been excluded from the Theosophical Society converted themselves into an Anthroposophical Society, which has continually increased its membership since then. Indeed, if we take into account the foolish calumnies directed so violently against the Anthroposophical Society and the lecturer in particular by the idol of the theosophists, Annie Besant, and by some of her idolizing followers, we can certainly not regard the separation of the Anthroposophical from the Theosophical Society as in any way a misfortune—especially if we also take into account many other things that since that time have emerged from the bosom of the Theosophical Society, supposedly as products of "the most noble philanthropy!"

Many readers of this cycle, who were at that time interested in the separation, will look upon the consequence of these battles, an echo of which appears here and there in these studies, as a kind of document that can be understood only in connection with the words that had to be spoken here. It may also be regarded as a demonstration of the manifold difficulties encountered by someone who believes he must defend something on purely factual grounds. However, if anyone does not agree with this viewpoint, he should be tolerant enough to skip, without resentment, those passages which in his opinion do not concern him. However, those for whose sake the lectures were given at the time they were delivered found in such passages a certain significance that should not be underestimated.

Rudolf Steiner.
Berlin, 1918

LECTURE 1

It is well known that the Gospel of St. Mark begins with the words: "This is the beginning of the Gospel of Jesus Christ."

A man of today who seeks to comprehend this Gospel of St. Mark is at once, in the very first words, faced with three riddles. The first is to be found in the words: "This is the beginning." The beginning of what? How can this beginning be understood? The second is: "the beginning of the Gospel . . ." In an anthroposophical sense, what does the word "Gospel" mean? The third riddle we have often spoken of: the figure of Christ Jesus Himself.

Whoever is seriously seeking for knowledge and a deepening of himself must recognize that mankind is evolving and progressing. For this reason what we may call the understanding of any revelation is not fixed once and for all, or confined to any particular epoch. It progresses, so that anyone who attaches a serious meaning to the terms "evolution" and "progress" must necessarily believe that as time goes on, mankind's deepest problems will be ever better, and more thoroughly and profoundly, understood. For something like the Gospel of St. Mark, as we shall demonstrate by means of these three riddles, a certain turning point in our comprehension has been reached only at the present time. Slowly and gradually, but distinctly, there has been prepared what can now lead us to a real understanding of the Gospel and enable us to understand that "the Gospel begins." Why is this the case?

We need only glance back a little to what filled human minds a comparatively short time ago and we shall see how

1

the very nature of comprehension may, indeed must, have altered in relation to a subject like this. If we go back further than the nineteenth century, we shall find that in the eighteenth and seventeenth centuries we approach ever closer to a time when those persons whose spiritual life was at all concerned with the Gospels had to start from a very different basis of comprehension than that of the man of today. What could an ordinary man of the eighteenth century say to himself if he wished to place himself in the general line of the evolution of humanity, and was not one of the few who were connected in some way with an initiation or some occult revelation—assuming that he had assimilated within himself everything offered by external exoteric life? Even the most cultivated man, one who stood on the highest pinnacle of the culture of his age, could not look back on more than three thousand years of the life of mankind; and one thousand of those years was before the Christian era and nearly lost in misty dimness. The other two thousand years since the founding of Christianity were not yet quite completed. He might look back three thousand years, shall we say? When one looked back at the earliest of these millennia one was confronted with a completely mythical, dim, prehistoric epoch of humanity, the age of old Persia. This, and what still remained of the knowledge of the ancient Egyptian epoch, preceded what "actual history" related, which began only with Hellenism. This Hellenism, to a certain extent, formed the foundation of the culture of this age. All those who wished to look more deeply into human life started with Hellenism; and within Hellenism appeared all that Homer, the Greek tragedians, and all the Greek writers have written concerning the primeval history of this people and their work for mankind.

Then one sees how Greece began to decline, how it was stifled by Rome, though only externally. Generally speaking, Rome overcame Greece only politically, while in reality it adopted Greek culture, Greek education and Greek life. It might be said that politically the Romans conquered the Greeks, but spiritually the Greeks conquered the Romans. During this latter process, while Hellenism was conquering Rome spiritually, it poured into Rome through hundreds and hundreds of channels what it had itself acquired. From Rome this streamed forth into all the other civilizations of the world, while during this time Christianity streamed more and more into the Greco-Roman civilization and was to a large extent transformed when the northern Germanic peoples took part in the spreading of the Greco-Roman Christian culture. With this intermingling of Greece, Rome, and Christianity, the second millennium of the world's history passed away, which to the men of the eighteenth century was the first Christian one. Then we see the beginning of the second Christian millennium, the third historical civilization of man. We see how everything goes on apparently in the same way, although, if we have deeper insight, we shall see that in this third millennium everything is really different. Two figures only need be cited, a painter and a poet, who, although they appear some two centuries after the end of the millennium, nevertheless show how something essentially new began for Western civilization with the second Christian millennium, something which these two men carried further. These two figures are Giotto and Dante. Giotto as painter and Dante as poet represent the beginning of all that followed, and what they gave was embodied in later Western cultures. Those were the three thousand years that could at that time be surveyed.

Then came the nineteenth century. Only someone who can look more deeply into the whole formation of the culture of the age is able now to perceive all that took place in the nineteenth century, and how for that reason everything had to become different. It is all contained in the minds and souls of men, but only a very few can as yet understand it.

3

The perspective of the man of the eighteenth century went back only to Hellenism; the age before that was somewhat nebulous. What happened in the nineteenth century—and this is little appreciated or understood today—is that the East played its part in the culture of the West, indeed very intensely so. This intervention of the Oriental influence in its own peculiar way is what we must bear in mind when considering the transformation that took place in the civilization of the nineteenth century. This penetration by the Orient threw light and shade upon everything that poured into the culture and will increasingly do so. For this reason a new understanding was required concerning things that up to that time humanity had regarded in a different light.

If we wish to choose single figures and individuals who have influenced the culture of the West, in whom we could find nearly everything that a man felt in his soul at the beginning of the nineteenth century if he concerned himself with spiritual life, we may mention David, Homer, Dante, Shakespeare, and Goethe, who was just beginning to penetrate into life. Future historians writing of the eighteenth and nineteenth centuries will be very clear about one thing, that the intellectual and spiritual life of that era was determined by these five figures. There lived then, more than anyone can imagine now, even in the most delicate stirrings of the soul, what we may call the feelings and truths of the Psalms. There lived also fundamentally what is to be found in Homer as well as what took such magnificent form in Dante; then, even if it did not live in Shakespeare himself, there was what is nevertheless so beautifully expressed by him in the form in which it now lives in men of modern times. Added to this is the striving of the human soul after truth which Goethe expressed in *Faust*, something that in reality lived in every human soul in such a way that it was often said, "Every man who seeks the truth has something of the Faust nature in him."

To all this there was added a quite new perspective, which exended beyond the three thousand years covered by these five persons. It came in ways that are at first quite un-fathomable by external history. This was the first entry of an inner Orient into the mental and spiritual life of Europe. It was not only that to the poems of those writers mentioned earlier was added what was given in the Vedas and the Bhaga-vad Gita, nor the fact that by learning to know these Eastern poems a different emotional nuance about the world was aroused, differing fundamentally from that of the Psalms or from what is to be found in the poetry of Dante or Homer, but something appeared in a mysterious manner which be-came ever more visible during the nineteenth century. One name alone will suffice, a name which made a great stir in the middle of the nineteenth century, and this will convince us that something came from the East to Europe along mys-terious paths. We need but mention the name of Schopen-hauer. In Schopenhauer what is it that strikes you most of all, if you leave aside the theoretical elements of his system? Isn't it the content of feeling and sentiment that pervades his whole thought? In the profound relationship between this nineteenth century man and the Oriental-Aryan mode of thought and feeling, in every sentence we might say, in the emphasis of feeling in Schopenhauer, lives that which we might call the Eastern element in the West; and this passed on to Eduard von Hartmann in the second half of the nineteenth century.

This penetrated along mysterious paths, as we have just said. We gradually come to better understand these mysteri-ous paths when we see that in the course of the develop-ments of the nineteenth century a complete transformation, a metamorphosis of all human thinking and feeling took place—not however in only one part of the earth but in the intellectual and spiritual life of the whole earth. As to what took place in the West, if anyone would take the trouble, it would be enough to compare anything written about religion, philosophy, or any aspect of spiritual life with something that belongs to the eighteenth century. He will then see that a complete transformation took place, that all the questions regarding the highest riddles asked by mankind had become more vague, that men were striving to formulate new questions, to look for new sentiments and modes of perception, that nothing belonging to religion and what it formerly gave to man could still be given through it to the human soul in the same way. Everywhere there was a longing for something deeper and more profoundly hidden in the depths of religion.

This was not true of Europe alone. It is characteristic of the beginning of the nineteenth century that all over the civilized world men, through an inner urge, were compelled to think differently. If we wish to form a more exact conception of what we are discussing, we must see that there was a general convergence of the peoples and their folk cultures and folk beliefs, with the result that people belonging to entirely different creeds began in the nineteenth century to understand each other in a quite remarkable way. We shall quote a characteristic example which lies at the heart of what we are trying to indicate. In the thirtieth year of the nineteenth century, a man appeared in England who was a Brahmin, an adherent of what he considered to be true Brahminism, that is, the Vedanta teaching. Ram Mohun Roy, who died in London in 1836, exercised a great influence on those of his contemporaries who were interested in such things, and made a great impression. The remarkable thing about him was that on the one hand he stood there as a reformer of Hinduism, though a misunderstood one, while on the other hand everything he said could be understood by all Europeans who were familiar with the advanced thought of their age. He did not put forth ideas that could be understood only through orientalism, but ideas that could be understood by ordinary human reason.

6

What was Ram Mohun Roy's attitude? He said something along these lines, "I live in the midst of Hinduism, where a number of different gods are worshipped. If the people of my country are asked why they worship these gods, they say, 'it is our custom, we know nothing else. It was done by our fathers and their fathers before them.' And because the people were influenced in this way," Ram Mohun Roy continued, "the crassest idolatry became the rule, an appalling idolatry which disgraces the original greatness of the religion of my fatherland. There once was a belief that, although partly contradictory, is to be found in the Vedas. It is the purest form of human thought, and it was brought into the Vedanta system by Viasa."

This was the belief professed by Ram Mohun Roy. For this reason he had not only made translations from various incomprehensible idioms into the languages that are understandable in India, but he also made extracts of what he considered the correct teaching and spread them among the people. What was his intention when he did this? He thought he recognized behind all that comes to expression in the various gods and all that is worshipped in the different idols a pure teaching of a primal divine unity, the spiritual God who lives in all things but can no longer be recognized in the idols. This God must once more penetrate into the minds of men. When this Indian Brahmin spoke in detail about what he believed to be the correct Vedanta teaching, the true Indian creed, it did not sound strange. To those who understood him rightly, it was as though he preached a kind of rational belief that can be attained by everyone who by using his rational mind turns to the universal unitary God. And Ram Mohun Roy had followers: Rabindranath Tagore and others. One of these followers, and this is especially interesting, gave a lecture in 1870 about Christ and Christianity. It was indeed extraordinarily interesting to hear an Indian speak about Christ and Christianity. The actual mystery of Christianity was quite remote from the Indian speaker—he did not touch upon that at all. From the whole course of the lecture we can see that he is quite unable to grasp the fundamental fact that Christianity does not proceed from a personal teacher but is founded on the Mystery of Golgotha, a world historical fact, on death and resurrection. But that which he can grasp and is so clear to him is that in Christ Jesus we have a figure of tremendous significance, one that is of importance to every human heart, a figure that must stand there as the ideal figure for the whole history of the world. It is remarkable to hear this Indian speaking about Christ and to hear him say, "If a man goes deeply into Christianity, he will see that Christianity must, even in the West, go through a further evolution, for what the European brings to my fatherland as Christianity does not appear to me to be the true Christianity."

We see from the examples quoted that it was not only in Europe that people's minds began to look behind the religious creeds, but also in distant India. It is true also of many parts of the earth where minds began to awake, and men approached in a new way and from an entirely new point of view something they had possessed for thousands of years. This metamorphosis of souls in the nineteenth century will be fully perceptible only in the course of time. Only in later times will history recognize that impulses of this kind, although apparently affecting only a few people, streamed through thousands of channels into our hearts and souls, so that today all those who participate in any way in spiritual life have them within their souls. This had to result in a total renewal. All older questions were transformed, and a new kind of understanding came into being in relation to all views that had hitherto been held. So it is that in the world, even today such questions are already taking on a greater profundity. What our spiritual movement desires today is the answering of these questions.

This spiritual movement is convinced that these questions cannot in their present form be answered by the old traditions, by modern natural science, or by that conception of the world which reckons only with the factors of modern natural science. Spiritual science, research into the spiritual worlds, is necessary. In other words, mankind today, in accordance with the whole trend of his evolution, must ask questions that can be answered only through supersensible investigation. Quite slowly and gradually there have emerged from the spiritual life of the West things that are once more in harmony with the most beautiful traditions that have come over from the East. You know that we have always stressed the fact that the law of reincarnation comes out of Western spiritual life itself, and that it need no more be taken as something historical coming from Buddhism than for example Pythagorean doctrine needs to be taken over from historical traditions. This has always been emphasized, but the fact that the idea of reincarnation arose in modern souls formed a bridge which extended across the three thousand years of which we have been speaking (during which the doctrine of reincarnation was not the center of thinking) to the figure of Buddha. The horizon, the perspective of the evolution of mankind, was extended beyond the three thousand years. This gave rise to new questions, which can be answered only through spiritual science.

Let us begin with the question to which the beginning of this Gospel of Saint Mark gives rise, this Gospel which begins with the words, "the beginning of the Gospel of Jesus Christ." Let us remember that these introductory words are immediately followed not only by a characterization of a passage of the old prophets but by the announcement of Christ by John the Baptist. This proclamation was stated by him in such a way that it may be comprised in these words: "The time is fulfilled; the kingdom of the divine is extending over the whole earth-existence." What does all this mean?

9

Let us endeavor with the light that modern spiritual science can give us to view retrospectively those past ages in the center of which is contained "the fulfillment." Let us try to understand what it means that "an old era is completed and a new one is beginning." We shall best be able to understand this if we first turn our attention to something belonging to more remote times and then consider something belonging to the modern era; between the two lies the Mystery of Golgotha. Let us take something before the Mystery of Golgotha and then something later, and then endeavor to enter deeply into the difference between the two epochs, so that we may recognize how far the old epoch had been completed and a new one begun. In this way we shall not enter into abstractions or definitions, but consider the concrete.

I should like you to turn your attention to the first millennium of human evolution, as it was thought to be in earlier times. There in the remotest period of this first millennium stands the towering figure of Homer, the Greek poet and singer. Hardly more than the name remains to mankind of him to whom are ascribed those two great poems which are among the greatest accomplishment of mankind: the Iliad and the Odyssey. Scarcely more than his name is known, and in the nineteenth century doubts were cast even on that —but we need not dwell any further on that now. The more we know of the figure of Homer, the more we admire him. For a person who studies such things, the characters created by Homer whom we meet in the Iliad and the Odyssey seem more alive than all the purely political figures of Greece. Many different people who have studied Homer over and over again have said that because of the precision of his descriptions and his manner of presentation he must have been a doctor. Others say he must have been an artist, a sculptor, or a craftsman. Napoleon admired the way Homer described tactics and strategy; still others think he must have been a beggar wandering through the land.

10

However all this may be, it certainly does demonstrate the unique individuality of Homer. Consider one of his characters, Hector. If you have any time available, you ought to study the figure of Hector in the Iliad—how plastically he is described so that he stands as a complete personality before us; how we see his affection for his paternal city, Troy, his wife Andromache, his relationship to Achilles, and to his armies; and how he commanded them. Try to call up this man before your minds, this man who possessed all the tenderness of a husband, and who clung in the ancient way to his home city of Troy, and who suffered such disillusions as only really great men can. Remember his relation with Achilles. Hector, as presented by Homer, is a towering figure from very ancient times, a man of great all-embracing humanity, for of course what Homer is describing belongs to a period well before his own, in the darkness of the past. Hector stands out above all the others, all those figures who seem mythical enough in the eyes of modern men.

Now take this one figure. Skeptics and all kinds of philologists may indeed doubt that there ever was a Hector at all, in the same way as they doubt the existence of Homer. But anyone who takes into consideration what may be understood from a purely human viewpoint will be convinced that Homer describes only facts that actually occurred. Hector was a living person who strode through Troy, and Achilles and the other figures were equally real. They still stand before us as personages of real earthly life. We look back to them as people of a different kind from ourselves, who are difficult to understand but whom the poet is able to bring before our souls in every detail. Now let us place before our souls a figure such as Hector, one of the chief Trojan commanders, who is defeated by Achilles. In such a personage we have something that belongs to the old pre-Christian age, something by which we can measure what men were before the time when Christ lived on earth.

I will now draw your attention to another figure, a

remarkable figure of the fifth century B.C.: the great philosopher Empedocles, who spent a large part of his life in Sicily. It was he who was the first to speak of the four elements, fire, water, air, and earth, and who said that everything that happens in the material realm caused by the mingling and disintegration of these four elements results from the principles of love and hate ruling in them. It was he also who by his activity influenced Sicily by calling into being important political institutions, and he went about trying to lead the people into a life of spirituality. When we look back to Empedocles we find that he lived an adventurous as well as a deeply spiritual life. Perhaps the truth of what I am about to say will be doubted by some, but spiritual science knows that Empedocles went about in Sicily not only as a statesman, but as a magician and initiate, just as Hector, as depicted by Homer, walked in Troy. In order to characterize the remarkable attitude of Empedocles toward the world the fact confronts us—and it is true and no invention—that in order, as it were, to unite himself with all existence around him, he ended by throwing himself into Mount Etna and was consumed by its fire. In this way a second figure of the pre-Christian age is presented to our souls.

Now let us consider such figures as these in accordance with the methods of spiritual science. First of all we know that these individualities will appear again; we know that such souls will return to life. We shall not pay any attention to their intermediate incarnations but look for them in the post-Christian era. We then see something of the change brought about by time, something that can help us to understand how the Mystery of Golgotha intervened in human evolution. If we say that such figures as Hector and Empedocles appeared again, we must ask how they walked among men in the post-Christian era. For we shall then see how the intervention of the Mystery of Golgotha, the fulfillment and beginning of a new age, worked on their souls. As serious

12

anthroposophists assembled here together we need not shrink from the communications of true spiritual science, which can be confirmed by external facts.

I should now like to turn your attention to something that took place in the post-Christian era, and perhaps again it may be said that the person concerned was a poetical personage. But this poetical personage can be traced back to a real individuality who was once alive. I direct your attention to the character created by Shakespeare in his Hamlet. Anyone who knows the development of Shakespeare, insofar as it can be known externally, and especially someone who is acquainted with it through spiritual science, will know that Shakespeare's Hamlet is none other than the transformed real prince of Denmark, who also lived at one time. I cannot go into everything underlying the historical prototype of the poetical figure of Hamlet, but through the research of spiritual science, I can offer you a striking example of how a man, a spirit of ancient times, reappears in the post-Christian era. The real figure underlying Hamlet, as presented by Shakespeare, is Hector. The same soul that lived in Hamlet lived in Hector. It is just by such a characteristic example as this, and the striking way the two different souls manifest themselves, that we can interpret what happened in the intervening time. A personality such as that of Hector stands before us in the pre-Christian age. Then comes the intervention of the Mystery of Golgotha in human evolution, and the spark it kindled in Hector's soul causes a figure, a prototype of Hamlet, to arise, of whom Goethe said, "This is a soul that is unable to deal with any situation and is not equal to its position, who is assigned tasks but is unable to fulfill them." We may ask why Shakespeare expressed it in this way. He did not know. But anyone who can investigate the connections through spiritual science knows that behind these things forces were at work. The poet creates in the unconscious; before him stands, so to speak, first the figure

13

which he creates, and then, as in a tableau of which he himself knows nothing, the whole individuality with which the figure is connected. Why does Shakespeare choose particular qualities in Hamlet and sharply emphasize them, qualities that perhaps Hamlet's own contemporaries would not have noticed? Because he observes them against the background of the era. He feels how different a soul has become in its transition from the old life to the new. Hamlet, the doubter, the skeptic, who has lost the ability to cope with the situations with which he meets in life, the procrastinator and waverer, this is what Hector, once so sure of himself, has become.

Let me direct your attention to another figure of modern times, who was also first presented to mankind in a poetic picture, in a poem whose protagonist will certainly live on in humanity for a long time to come when for posterity the poet, like Homer or Shakespeare, no longer is in existence. About Homer we know nothing at all, and about Shakespeare we know very little indeed. What the various compilers of notes and biographers of Goethe have written will long since have been forgotten. In spite of the printing press and other modern inventions, what interests people in Goethe at the present time will likewise have been long forgotten. But large as life, and modelled from life, there will stand the figure of Faust which Goethe has created. Just as men today know nothing of Homer, so will they some day know but little of Goethe (which will be a good thing); but they will know much about Faust. Faust again is a figure who, as he is presented to us in a literary form by Goethe, can be recognized as one brought to a certain conclusion by Goethe. The poetical picture refers back to a real sixteenth century figure who lived then as a real person, though he was not as Goethe described him in his *Faust*. Why then did Goethe describe him in this way? Goethe himself did not know. But when he directed his attention to the traditional Faust that had been

14

handed down to him, a Faust with whom he was already acquainted through the marionettes of his boyhood, then the forces that stood behind Faust, the forces of his previous incarnation, the forces of Empedocles, the old Greek philosopher, worked within him! All these radiated into the figure of Faust. So we might say, since Empedocles threw himself into Etna and united himself with the fire-element of the earth, what a wonderful spiritualization of pre-Christian nature mysticism was accomplished in fact in the final tableau of Goethe's *Faust*, when Faust ascends into the fire-element of heaven through Pater Seraphicus and the rest. Slowly and gradually a totally new spiritual tendency entered into the deeper strivings of men. Already some time ago it began to become evident to the more profound spirits of mankind that, without their knowing anything about reincarnation or karma, when they were considering a great comprehensive soul whom they wished to describe from the depths of their inner life, they found themselves describing what radiated over from earlier incarnations. Although Shakespeare did not know that Hamlet was Hector, he nevertheless described him as such, without being aware that the same soul had lived in both of them. So too Goethe portrays his Faust as though Empedocles with all his peculiarities were standing behind him, because in his Faust there lived the soul of Empedocles. It is characteristic that the progress of the human soul should proceed in this way.

I have mentioned two characteristic figures, in both of whom we can perceive that when great men of earlier times reappear in a modern post-Christian age, they are shaken to the very depths of their souls and can only with difficulty adjust themselves to life. Everything that was within them in the past is still within them. For example, when we allow Hamlet to work upon us, we feel that the whole force of Hector is in him. But we feel that this force cannot come forth in the post-Christian era, that it then meets with

15

obstacles, that something now works upon the soul that is the beginning of something new, whereas in the figures of antiquity something was coming to an end. So do these figures stand plastically delineated before us; both Hector and Empedocles represent a conclusion. But what is working on further in mankind must find new paths into new incarnations. This is revealed with Hector in Hamlet and also with Empedocles in Faust, who had within him all the abysmal urges toward the depths of nature. Because he had within him the whole nature of Empedocles, he could say, "I will lay aside the Bible for a time and study nature and medicine. I will no longer be a theologian." He felt the need to have dealings with demonic beings who made him roam through the world leaving him marveling but uncomprehending. Here the Empedocles element had an after-effect but was not able to adjust itself to what a man must be after the new age had begun.

I wanted to show you through these explanations how in well-known souls, about whom anyone can find information, a powerful transformation shows itself, and how the more deeply we study them the more perceptible this becomes. If we inquire what happened between the two incarnations of such individualities, the answer always is the Mystery of Golgotha, which was announced by the Baptist when he said, "The time is fulfilled, the kingdoms of the spirit, or the kingdoms of heaven, are passing over into the kingdom of man." Yes, the kingdoms of heaven did indeed powerfully seize the human kingdom, but those who take this in an external sense are unable to understand it. They seized it so powerfully that the great men of antiquity, who had been in themselves so solid and compact, had to make a new beginning in human evolution on earth. This new beginning showed itself precisely with them, and lasted until the end of the old epoch, with the Mystery of Golgotha. At that time something that had been fulfilled ebbed away, something which had presented men in such a way that they appeared as rounded personalities in themselves. Then came something that made it necessary for these souls to make a new beginning. Everything had to be transformed and altered so that great souls appeared small. They had to be transformed into the stage of childhood, for something quite new was beginning. We must inscribe this in our souls if we wish to understand what is meant at the beginning of the Gospel of St. Mark by the words "a beginning." Yes, truly a beginning, a beginning that shakes the inmost soul to its foundations and brings a totally new impulse into human evolution, a "beginning of the Gospel."

What then is the Gospel? It is something that comes down to us from the kingdoms we have often described, where dwell the higher hierarchical beings, among whom are the angels and archangels. It descends through the world that rises above the human world. So do we gain an inkling of the deeper meaning of the word Gospel. It is an impulse that descends through the realms of the archangels and angels; it comes down from these kingdoms and enters into mankind. None of the abstract translations really covers the matter adequately. In reality the word Gospel should indicate that at a certain time something begins to flow in upon the earth which formerly flowed only where there dwell the angels and archangels. Something descended to earth that shook the souls of men and shook the strongest souls most. It is here noted that this was the beginning, and the beginning has a continuation. The beginning was made at that time, and we shall see that fundamentally the whole development of humanity since then is a continuation of that beginning when the impulse began to flow down from the kingdom of the *angeloi*, or what we call the "ev-angel" or Gospel.

We cannot seek or investigate deeply enough if we wish to characterize the different Gospels. We shall see that especially the Gospel of St. Mark can be understood only if we understand in the right way the evolution of humanity with all its impulses and all that has happened in the course of it. I do not wish to describe this externally, but to characterize actual souls, showing how it is only the recognition of the fact of reincarnation, when it becomes a matter of real research, that can bear witness to the progress of such souls as those of Hector and Empedocles. Only in this way can the deeper significance of the Christ Impulse be brought before our souls. Otherwise we may discover beautiful things, but they will all be superficial. What lies behind all the outer events in the history of the Christ Impulse is discovered only when we can throw light upon life through spiritual research, so that we can recognize how a single life passes not only in its separate phases but also in the sequence of incarnations. We must look upon reincarnation as a serious matter and apply it to history in such a way that it becomes an element that gives life to it. We shall then perceive the working of the Event of Golgotha, the greatest of all impulses. It is especially in souls that this impulse, which we have described often enough, will become visible.

LECTURE 2

If you recollect what was to a certain extent the climax and principal goal of our last lecture, you will be able to place before your souls how completely different the human entity was as regards his innermost self before the Mystery of Golgotha from what it was after that event. I did not try to put general characteristics before you, but examples from spiritual science, examples that showed us souls of olden times and souls belonging to modern times, characteristic examples by means of which we can see how certain souls of former times appear again, transformed and metamorphosed. The reason for such a great change will become evident only from the study of the whole course of these lectures. But at present one thing only may be pointed out by way of introduction, which has often been referred to in our lectures when they touched on similar subjects, namely, that the full consciousness of the human ego, which it is the mission of the earth planet to develop and bring to expression, actually made its appearance only through the Mystery of Golgotha.

It is not perhaps quite accurate, though not far wrong, to say that if we go very far back in evolution, human souls were not yet truly individualized; they were still entangled in the group-soul nature. This was particularly the case with the more prominent among them, so we may say that such natures as Hector or Empedocles were typical group-soul representatives of their entire human community. Hector grew out of the soul of Troy. He stands as an image of the group soul of the Trojan people in a particular form, specialized but nevertheless just as rooted in the group soul as Empedocles. When they were reincarnated in the post-Chris-

19

tian era, they had to face the necessity of experiencing the ego-consciousness. This passing over from the group-soul nature to the experience of the individual soul causes a mighty leap forward. It causes souls so firmly embedded in the group-soul nature as Hector to appear like Hamlet, i.e. wavering and uncertain, as though incapable of dealing with life. On the other hand it causes a soul like that of Empedocles, when it reappears in post-Christian times as the soul of the Faust of the sixteenth century, to become a kind of adventurer who is brought into various situations from which he was only with difficulty able to extricate himself, and who is misunderstood by his contemporaries and even by posterity.

Indeed, it has often been emphasized that in developments such as those here referred to, all that has taken place since the Mystery of Golgotha is not particularly meaningful. As yet everything is only at the beginning; only during the future evolution of the earth will the great impulses that may be ascribed to Christianity make themselves felt. Over and over again we must emphasize the fact that Christianity is only at the beginning of its great development. If we wish to play a part in this great development, we must enter with understanding into the ever increasing progress of the revelations and impulses which originated with the founding of Christianity. Above all we are required to learn something in the immediate future; for it does not take much clairvoyance to see clearly that if we wish for something definite to enable us to make a good beginning in the direction of an advanced and progressive understanding of Christianity, we must learn to read the Bible in quite a new way. There are at present many hindrances in the way, partly because of the fact that in wide circles biblical study is still carried on in a sugary and sentimental manner. The Bible is not made use of as a book of knowledge, but as a book of common use for all kinds of personal situations. If anyone has need of it for his own personal encouragement,

20

he will bury himself in one or the other chapter of the Bible and allow it to work on him. This seldom results in anything more than a personal relationship to the Bible. On the other hand, the scholarship of the last decades, indeed that of virtually the whole nineteenth century, increased the difficulty of really understanding the Bible by tearing it apart, declaring that the New Testament is composed of all kinds of different things that were later combined, and that the Old Testament also was composed of many different parts which must have been brought together at different times. According to this view, the Bible is made up of mere fragments which may easily produce the impression of an aggregate, presumably stitched together in the course of time. This kind of scholarship has become popular; very many people, for example, hold that the Old Testament is combined out of many single parts. This opinion disturbs the serious reading of the Bible that must come in the near future. When such a serious way of reading the Bible is adopted, all that is to be said about its secrets from the anthroposophical viewpoint will be much better understood.

For example, we must learn to take as a whole the Old Testament from the beginning up to the point where the ordinary editions of the Bible end. We must not let ourselves be led astray by all that may be said against the unity of the Old Testament. Then, if we do not merely read it in a one-sided way seeking for personal edification, and do not read one part or another from any particular point of view, but allow the Old Testament, just as it is, to influence us as a whole, combining our consideration of the contents with all that must come into the world precisely from our anthroposophical development of the last few years—if we unite all this with a certain artistic spiritual feeling so that we gradually come to see the artistic sequence, how the threads interweave and are disentangled, not as if it had been composed in an external kind of way, but with deep artistry, then we shall gradually perceive what a mighty, inwardly spiritual dramatic power lies in the whole structure and composition of the Old Testament. Only then do we appreciate the glorious tableau as a uniform whole, and we shall no longer believe that one piece in the middle comes from one source and one from another. We shall then perceive the unitary spirit of the Bible. We shall see how from the first day of creation the continuity of progress is under the control of this unitary spirit from the time of the patriarchs through the time of the judges, and through that of the great Jewish prophets and kings until the whole soars to a wonderful dramatic culmination in the book of the Maccabees, in the sons of Mattathias, the brothers of Judas who fought against the king of Antioch. In the whole there lives an inner dramatic force that reaches a certain culminating point at the end. We shall then feel that it is not a mere phrase when we say that a man who is equipped with the occult method of observation is seized by a peculiar feeling when he comes to the end of the Old Testament and has in front of him the seven sons of the Maccabean mother and the five sons of Mattathias. Five sons of Mattathias, with the seven sons of the Maccabean mother making the remarkable number twelve, a number we notice everywhere when we are led into the secrets of evolution.

The number twelve appears at the end of the Old Testament as the culminating point of the whole dramatic presentation. First this feeling comes upon us when the seven sons of the Maccabees die a martyr's death, how one by one they rise up and one by one are martyred. Observe the inner dramatic power shown here, how the first victim only hints at what comes to full expression in the seventh in his belief in the immortality of the soul, how he hurls these words at the king, "You reprobate, you refuse to hear anything about the Awakener of my soul." (Macc. 2:7.) If we allow the dramatic crescendo of power from son to son to affect us, we shall see what forces are contained in the Bible. If we compare the sugary sentimental method of study prevalent hitherto with this dramatic, artistic penetration, the Bible is of itself able to arouse religious ardor. Here, through the Bible, art becomes religion. And then we begin to notice very remarkable things. Most of you may perhaps remember, for it happened in this very place, that when I gave here the course on St. Luke's Gospel the whole magnificent figure of Christ Jesus sprang forth from the fusion of the two souls, the souls of the two Jesus children. The soul of the one was none other than the soul of Zarathustra, the founder of Zoroastrianism. You may still have before your spiritual eyes the fact that in the Jesus boy described in the Gospel of St. Matthew is the reincarnated Zarathustra.

What kind of fact do we have here? We have the founder of Zoroastrianism, the great initiate of antiquity, of the primeval Persian civilization, who passed through human evolution up to a certain point and appeared again among the ancient Hebrew people. Through the soul of Zarathustra, we have a transition from the ancient Persian to the element of the ancient Hebrew people. Yes indeed, the external, that which takes place in the history of the world and in human life, is really only the manifestation, the externalization of inner spiritual processes and of inner spiritual forces. What external history relates can therefore be studied by considering it as an expression of the inward and spiritual, of the facts which move in the spiritual realm. Let us place before our souls the fact that Zarathustra passed over from Persia into the old Hebrew element. Now let us consider the Old Testament—we really only need to study the headings of the chapters. That the matter stands with Zarathustra as I then related is the result of clairvoyant research: it results if we follow his soul backward in time. Now let us contrast this result not only with the way the Bible represents it, but also with the results of external investigation.

The ancient Hebrew people founded their kingdom in Palestine. That original kingdom was divided. First it passed into Assyrian captivity, then into the Babylonian. The ancient Hebrew people were subjugated by the Persians. What does all this mean? World historical facts do indeed have a meaning; they correspond with inner processes, spiritual soul-processes. Why did all this take place? Why were the ancient Hebrew people guided in such a way that they passed over into the Chaldean, into the Assyrian-Babylonian element, and were set free again by Alexander the Great?* To put it briefly, it is because this was merely the external transition of Zarathustra from the Persian to the Jewish element. The Jews brought him to themselves. They were guided to him, even being subjugated by the Persian element, because Zarathustra wanted to come to them. External history is a wonderful counterpart of these processes, and anyone who observes these things from the point of view of spiritual science knows that external history was only the body for the transition of the Zarathustra element from the old Persian element, which at first actually included the old Hebrew element. Then, when the latter had been sufficiently permeated by the Persian element, it was lifted out of it again by Alexander the Great. What then remained was the milieu

---

*The Israelites in Babylon were of course allowed by Cyrus to go home after his conquest of that city, and his Persian successors followed the same policy (II Chron. 36:22, Ezra I. See also the rest of the book of Ezra, Nehemiah, and Haggai, especially for the rebuilding of the temple). However, if the paragraph is taken as a whole, it seems evident that Steiner was thinking of the general dispersion of the Jews in the Hellenistic world in the centuries following the conquests of Alexander, a dispersion that in the end provided a suitable milieu for the reborn Zarathustra. As far as is known to history, Alexander himself did not play any significant part in the liberation of the Jews. (Editorial note.)

necessary for Zarathustra; it had passed over from one people to another.

When we glance over this whole age—we can naturally emphasize only a few single points—we see it reaching its apex in the old Hebrew history, through the period of the kings, the prophets, the Babylonian captivity, and the Persian conquest up to the time of the Maccabees. If then we really wish to understand the Gospel of St. Mark, which is ushered in by one of the prophetic sayings of Isaiah, we cannot fail to be struck by the element of the Jewish prophets. Starting from Elijah, who reincarnated as John the Baptist, we could say that these prophets appear to us in their wonderful grandeur. Let us leave out of consideration for the moment Elijah and his reincarnation as the Baptist, and consider the names of the intervening prophets. Here we must say that what we have obtained from spiritual science allows us to observe these Jewish prophets in a very special way. When we speak of the great spiritual leaders of the earth in ancient times, to whom do we refer? To the initiates, the initiated ones. We know that these initiates attained their spiritual height precisely because they went through the various stages of consecration. They raised themselves stage by stage by means of cognition to spiritual vision, and thus to union with the true spiritual impulses in the world. In this way they were able to embody in the life of the physical plane the impulses they themselves received in the spiritual world. When we meet with an initiate of the Persian, Indian, or Egyptian people our first question is, "How did he ascend the ladder of initiation within his own national environment? How did he become a leader, and thus a spiritual guide of his people?"

This question is everywhere justifiable, except when we come to the prophets. At the present time, there is certainly a sort of theosophical tendency to mix everything together

25

and speak about the prophets in the same way as we speak of other initiates. But nothing can be known by doing this. Let us take the Bible (and recent historical research shows that the Bible is a true and not an untrue document); consider the prophets from Isaiah to Malachi, through Jeremiah, Ezekiel, and Daniel, and study what it relates of these figures. You will find that you cannot bring these prophets into the general scheme of intitiation. Where does the Bible relate that the Jewish prophets went through the same kind of initiation as other initiates belonging to different peoples? It is said they appeared when the voice of God stirred in their souls, enabling them to see in a different way from ordinary men, making it possible for them to make indications as to the future course of the destiny of their people and the future course of the world's history. Such indications were wrung from the souls of the prophets with elemental force. It is not related of them, in the same way as it is related of other prophets, how they went through their initiation. The spiritual vision of the Jewish prophets seems, so to speak, to spring from their own genius, and this they relate to their own people and to humanity. It was in this same way that they avowed their prophesies and acknowledged their prophetic gifts. Just consider how a prophet, when he has something to announce, always makes a point of proclaiming that God has communicated through some mediator what is to happen—or else that it came to him like a direct elemental truth. This gives rise to the question, leaving Elijah and his reincarnation as the Baptist out of consideration, "What position do these Jewish prophetic figures occupy, who externally are placed side by side with the initiates of other nations?" If you investigate the souls of these prophets in the light of spiritual science or occultism, you come to something very remarkable. If you make the effort to compare what history and religious tradition relate with what I am about to communicate to you as the result of my spiritual investigation, you will be able to verify this.

26

We find that the souls of the Hebrew prophets are rein-
carnations of initiates who had lived in other nations, and
who had attained certain stages of initiation. When we trace
backward one of these prophets, we arrive at some other
people and find an initiated soul who remained a long time
with this people. This soul then went through the portal of
death and was reincarnated in the Jewish people. If we wish
to find the earlier incarnations of the souls of Jeremiah,
Isaiah, Daniel, and so on, we must seek them among other
peoples. Trivially speaking, it is as though there were a
gradual assembling of the initiates of other peoples among
the Jewish people, where these initiates appear in the form
of prophets. This is why these prophets appear in such a
way that their gift of prophecy appears to proceed elemen-
tally from out of their own inner being. It is a memory of
what they acquired here or there as initiates. All this emerges,
but not always in the harmonious form it had in earlier incarnations, for a soul that had been incarnated in a Persian
or Egyptian body would first have to accustom itself to the
bodily nature of the Jewish people. Something of what was
certainly in this soul could not come forth in this incarnation. For it is not always the case that what a man has formerly acquired reappears in him as he progresses from
incarnation to incarnation. Indeed, through the difficulties
caused by the bodily nature, it may come forth in an inhar-
monious way, in a chaotic manner.

Thus we see that the Jewish prophets gave their people
many spiritual impulses, which are often disarrayed, but
nonetheless grandiose recollections of former incarnations.
That is the peculiarity to be observed in the Jewish prophets.
Why is this? It is because in fact the whole evolution of
humanity had to go through this passageway, so that what
was achieved in its parts over the whole world should be
brought together in one focal point, to be born again from
out of the blood of the people of the Old Testament. So we
find in the history of the old Hebrew people, as in that of no

other, something that may be found also in tribes but not in peoples that had already become nations—a state of homogenity, the emphasizing of the descent of the blood through the generations. All that belongs to the world-historical mission of the Old Testament people depends upon the continuity of the stream of blood through the generations. Hence anyone who had a full right to belong to the Jewish people was always called a ''son of Abraham, Isaac, and Jacob,'' meaning a son of that element that first appeared in the blood of Abraham, Isaac and Jacob. It was in the blood that flowed through this people that the elements of initiation of other peoples were to reincarnate. Like rays of light coming from different sides, streaming in and uniting in the center, the incarnating rays of the various peoples were collected together as in one central point in the blood of the old Hebrew people. The psychical element of human evolution had once to pass through that experience. It is extremely important to keep these occult facts in mind, for only thus can we understand how such a Gospel as that of St. Mark is from its beginning based upon the element of the Old Testament.

But now what occurs at this gathering, as we might call it, of the initiation elements of the various peoples in this one center? We have yet to see why it took place. But if we now take the whole dramatic progress of the Old Testament into consideration, we shall see how the thought of immortality is gradually developed in the Old Testament through the taking up of the initiation elements of the different peoples and how it appears at its very summit precisely in the sons of the Maccabees. But we must now allow this to influence our souls in its full original significance, enabling us to envision the consciousness man then had of his connection with the spiritual world. I wish to draw your attention to one thing. Try to follow up the passages in the Old Testament where reference is made to the divine element shining into human life. How often it is related, for example in the Book of Tobit (Tobit 5), when something or other is about to happen—as when Tobit sends his son to carry out some business or other—the archangel Raphael appears to him in an apparently human form.* In another passage other beings of the higher hierarchies appear. Here we have the divine spiritual element playing into the world of man in such a way that man sees the divine spiritual element as something external, met with in the outer world. In the Book of Tobit, Raphael confronts the person he has to lead in just the same way as one man encounters another when he approaches him externally. We shall often see if we study the Old Testament that connections with the spiritual world are regulated in this manner, and very many passages in the Old Testament refer to something of this kind. But as we proceed, we observe a great dramatic progression, finally reaching the culminating point of that progression in the martyrdom of the seven sons of the Maccabees who speak out of their souls of a uniting, a reawakening of their souls in the divine element. The inner certainty of soul about their own inner immortality meets us in the sons of the Maccabees and also in Judas and his brothers who were to defend their people against the king of Antioch. There is an increased inner understanding of the divine spiritual element, and the dramatic progress becomes ever greater as we follow the Old Testament from the appearance of God to Moses in the burning bush, in which we see God approaching man externally, to the inner certitude springing up in the souls of the sons of the Maccabees, who are convinced that if they die here they will be reawakened in the kingdom of their God through what lives within them.

---

*The reference is to the wonderful journey by Tobias, the son of Tobit, who goes to a far land to bring back a wife after he has freed her from a demon. He does this with the aid of Raphael who also shows him how to cure his father of blindness.

This shows a mighty progression, revealing an inner unity in the Old Testament. Nothing is said at the beginning of the Old Testament concerning the consciousnes of being accepted by God, of being taken away from the earth and being part of the Divinity. Nor are we told whether this member of the human soul that is taken up by God and embodied in the divine world is really raised. But the whole progress was so guided that the consciousness develops more and more, so that the human soul through its very essence grows into the spiritual element. From a state of passivity toward the God Yahweh or Jehovah, there gradually comes into being an active inner consciousness of the soul about its own nature. This increases page by page all through the Old Testament, though it was only by slow degrees that during its progress the thought of immortality was born. Strange to say, the same progress may also be observed in the succession of the prophets. Just observe how the stories and predictions of each successive prophet become more and more spiritual; here again we find the dramatic element of a wonderful intensification. The further we go back into the past, the more do the stories told relate to the external. The more we advance in time, the more we discover the inner force, the inner certainty and feeling of unity with the divine spiritual, referred to also by the prophets. Thus there is a continual enhancement until the Old Testament leads on to the beginning of the story of the New Testament, and the Gospel of St. Mark is directly linked with all this.

For at the very beginning, the Gospel tells us that it intends to interpret the event of Christ Jesus entirely in the sense of the old prophets, so that it is possible to understand the appearance of Christ Jesus by keeping before us the words of Malachi and Isaiah respectively, "Behold I send my messenger before you who is to prepare the way. Hear how there is a cry in the wilderness, 'Prepare the way of the Lord and make his paths level.' " Thus there is a prevailing tone running through the history of the Old Testament pointing to the appearance of Christ Jesus. It is further related in St. Mark's Gospel—indeed we may distinctly hear it in the words if we so desire. In the same way that the ancient prophets spoke, so essentially does the Baptist speak. How comprehensive and grandiose is this figure of the Baptist if we interpret him in the way the ancient prophets spoke of a divine messenger, of one who in the solitude would show the path that Christ Jesus had to pursue in cosmic evolution. Mark's Gospel then goes on to say, "Thus does John the Baptist appear in the solitude and proclaim baptism for the recognition of human sinfulness." For in this way should the words rightly be translated. So it is said, "Direct your gaze to the old prophetic nature, which has now entered into a new relation with the Divinity and experienced a new belief in immortality. And then behold the figure of the Baptist, how he appeared and spoke of the kind of development through which we may recognize the sinfulness of man." Thus is the Baptist directly referred to as a great figure.

But how about the wonderful figure of Christ Jesus Himself? Nowhere else in the world is He presented in so simple and at the same time so grand and dramatic an ascending gradation as in Mark's Gospel. Direct your spiritual gaze at this in the right way. What are we told at the beginning of the Gospel? We are particularly told to turn our attention to the figure of the Baptist. You can understand him only when you take into account the Jewish prophets, whose voice has become alive in him. The whole Jewish nation went up to be baptized by him. This means that there were many among them who recognized that the old prophets spoke through John the Baptist. That is stated at the beginning of the Gospel. We see John standing before us, we hear the voice of the old prophets coming to life in him, and we see the people going out to him and recognizing him as a prophet come to life again. Let us confine ourselves for the moment to the Mark Gospel. Now the figure of Christ Jesus Himself appears. Let us now also leave out of account the so-called baptism in the Jordan, and what happens after that, including the temptation, and fix our attention on the dramatic intensification we meet with in the Mark Gospel.

After the Baptist is introduced to us, and we are shown how the people regard him and his mission, Christ Jesus is Himself introduced. But in what manner? At first we are told only that He is there, that He is recognized not only by men, but He is also recognized by beings other than man. That is the point to be borne in mind. Around Him are those who wish to be healed from their demonic possession, those in whom demons are active. Around Him stand men in whom not merely human souls are living, but who are possessed by supersensible spirits who work through them. And in a significant passage we are told that these spirits recognize Christ Jesus. Of the Baptist we are told that men recognized him and went out to be baptized by him. But Christ is recognized by the supersensible spirits, so that He has to command them not to speak of Him. Beings from the supersensible world recognize Him, so it is said; that being is entering who is not only recognized by men, but His appearance is recognized and considered dangerous by supersensible beings. That is the glorious climax confronting us directly in the beginning of the Gospel of Mark. On the one side is John the Baptist, recognized and honored by men; and on the other He who is recognized and feared by supersensible beings—who nevertheless have something to do with the earth—so that they realize that now they must leave. Nowhere else is such an upward dramatic progression presented with such simplicity.

If we keep this in sight, we feel certain things as necessary which usually simply pass unobserved by human souls. Let me draw your attention to a particular passage which, because of the greatness and simplicity of Mark's Gospel, may best be observed in this Gospel. Recall the passage in which the choosing of the Twelve is spoken of at the beginning of the Gospel, and how, when the naming is referred to, it is said that He called two of His apostles the "sons of thunder" (Mark 3: 17). That is a fact that must not pass unnoticed; we must pay attention to it if we wish to understand the Gospel. Why does He call them "sons of thunder?" Because He wishes to implant into them an element that is not of the earth so that they may become His servants. This element comes from outside the earth because this is the Gospel that comes from the world of angels and archangels. It is something new; it is no longer enough to speak of man. He speaks now of a heavenly supersensible element, the ego, and it is necessary to emphasize this. He calls them sons of thunder to show that those who are His followers are related to the celestial element. The nearest world connected with our own is the elemental world, through which what plays into our world can first be explained. Christ gives names to His disciples which indicate that our world borders on a supersensible one. He gives them names in accordance with the characteristics of the elemental world. It is just the same as when He calls Peter the "rock-man" (3: 16). This again refers to the supersensible. Thus through the whole Gospel the entrance of the angelic as an impulse from the spiritual world is proclaimed.

In order to understand this we only need to read correctly, and assume that the Gospel is at the same time a book from which the deepest wisdom can be drawn. All the progress that has been made consists in this: souls are becoming individualized. They are connected with the supersensible world not only indirectly through their group-soul nature, but they are also connected with it through the element of the individual soul. He who so stands before humanity that He is recognized by the beings of earth and is also recognized by supersensible beings needs the best element of human nature to enable Him to sink something of the supersensible into the souls of those who are to serve Him. He requires such men as have themselves made the furthest progress in their souls according to the old way. It is extremely interesting to follow the soul-development of those whom Christ Jesus gathered around Him; the Twelve whom He particularly called to be His own, who, in all their simplicity, as we might say, passed in the grandest way through the development which, as I tried to show you yesterday, is gained by human souls in widely varied incarnations.

A man must first become accustomed to being a specific individuality. This he cannot easily do when he is transferred from the element of the nation in which his soul had taken root into a condition of being dependent upon himself alone. The Twelve were deeply rooted in a nationality which had constituted itself in the grandest form. They stood there as if they were naked souls, simple souls, when Christ found them again. There had been a quite abnormal interval between their incarnations. The gaze of Christ Jesus could rest upon the Twelve, the reincarnated souls of those who had been the seven sons of the Maccabean and the five sons of Mattathias, Judas and his brothers; it was of these that the apostolate was formed. They were thrown into the element of fishermen and simple folk. But at a time when the Jewish element had reached its culminating point they had been permeated by the consciousness that this element was then at the peak of its strength, but strength only —whereas, when the group formed itself around Christ, this element appeared in individualized form. We might conceive that someone who was a complete unbeliever might look upon the appearance of the seven and the five at the end of the Old Testament, and their reappearance at the beginning of the New Testament, as nothing but an artistic progression. If we take it as a purely artistic composition, we may be moved by its simplicity and the artistic greatness of the Bible, quite apart from the fact that the Twelve are the five sons of Mattathias and the seven sons of the Maccabean mother. And we must learn to take the Bible also as a work of art. Then only shall we develop a feeling for the artistic element in it, and acquire a feeling for the realities from which it springs.

Now perhaps your attention may be called to something else. Among the five sons of Mattathias is one who is already called Judas in the Old Testament. He was the one who at that time fought more bravely than all the others for his own people. In his whole soul he was dedicated to his people, and it was he who was successful in forming an alliance with the Romans against King Antiochus of Syria (I Macc: 8). This Judas is the same who later had to undergo the test of the betrayal, because he who was most intimately bound up with the old specifically Hebrew element, could not at once find the transition into the Christian element, needing the severe testing of the betrayal. Again, if we look at the purely artistic aspect, how wonderfully do the two figures stand out: the grand figure of the Judas in the last chapters of the Old Testament and the Judas of the New Testament. It is remarkable that in this symptomatic process, the Judas of the Old Testament concluded an alliance with the Romans, prefiguring all that happened later, namely the path that Christianity took through the Roman Empire, so that it could enter into the world. If I could add to this something that can also be known but that cannot be given in a lecture to an audience as large as this, you would see that it was precisely through a later reincarnation of Judas that the fusion of the Roman with the Christian element occurred. The reincarnated Judas was the first who, as we might say, had the great success of spreading Romanized Christianity in the world. The treaty concluded by the Judas of the Old Testament with the Romans was the prophetic foreshadowing of what was later accomplished by another man, who is recognized by occultists as the reincarnation of that Judas who had to go through the severe soul-testing of the betrayal. What through his later influence appears as Christianity within Romanism and Romanism within Christianity is like a renewal of the alliance concluded between the Old Testament Judas and the Romans, but transferred into the spiritual.

When we have such things as these before us, we gradually come to the conclusion that, considered spiritually and leaving everything else aside, human evolution is itself the greatest work of art that has ever existed; only we must have the vision to see it. Ought it therefore to be regarded as so unreasonable to look at the human soul in this way? I think if we contemplate one or the other of these dramas with their clear raveling and unraveling, while lacking the capacity for perceiving its structure, we shall see nothing but a sequence of events following one after another. External history is written somewhat in this way. Seen thus, human evolution does not appear as a work of art; nothing emerges but a succession of events. But mankind is now at a turning point when it must interpret the inner progressive shaping of events, their raveling and unraveling in the evolution of humanity. Then it will appear that the evolution of humanity clearly and distinctly shows how individual figures appear at definite times and give impulses while entangling or unraveling the plot. We only learn to understand how man is inserted into human evolution when we come to know the course of history in this way. But because it is all raised from the condition of a mere joining together to that of an organism, and then to more than an organism, everything must really be put in its proper place and the distinctions made that in other domains are taken for granted. It would not occur to any astronomer to equate the sun to the other planets. He would as a matter of course keep it separate and single it out as a separate entity within the planetary system. In the same way, a man who sees into human evolution places a "sun" as a matter of course among the great leaders of humanity. Just as it would be utter nonsense to speak of the sun of our planetary system as being on a par with Venus, Jupiter, or Mars, so it would be nonsense to speak of Christ in the same way as the Boddhisattvas or other leaders of humanity. This should be so obvious that the very idea of a reincarnation of Christ would be ridiculous, and such an assertion could not be made if things were simply looked at as they are. But it is necessary really to go into the questions and grasp them in their proper form, and not to accept the dogma of any sectarian belief. When we speak of Christology in a true cosmological sense, it is not necessary to show a preference for the Christian above any other religion. That would be the same as if some religion in its sacred writings stated that the sun was the same as the other planets, and then someone came along and said, "No, we must place the sun higher than the other planets, and some people opposed this by saying, "But this is favoritism toward the sun!" This is not favoritism, it is only recognizing the truth.

So it is also in the case of Christianity. It is simply a question of recognizing the truth, a truth that every religion on the earth today could accept if it chose to do so. If other religions are in earnest in their tolerance for all other religious creeds and do not use that tolerance as a pretense, they will not object that the West has not adopted a national god, but a God in whom no nationality plays a part, a God who is a cosmic being. The Indians speak of their national gods. As a matter of course their ideas differ from those of people who have not adopted a Germanic national god, but accept as a God a Being who was, to be sure, never incarnated in their own land, but in a distant land and in a different nation. We might perhaps speak of a Western-Christian principle in opposition to an Indian-Eastern one, if we wished to put Wotan above Krishna. But that is not the case with Christ.

From the beginning He belonged to no nation but stood for the truth of the most beautiful of the spiritual scientific principles, "to recognize the truth without distinction of color, race, nationality, etc."

We must acquire the capacity to look at these things objectively. Only when we recognize the Gospels by recognizing what underlies them shall we truly understand them. From what has been said today about the Mark Gospel in its sublime simplicity and its dramatic crescendo from the person of John the Baptist to that of Christ Jesus, we can see what this Gospel actually contains.

LECTURE 3

In the last lecture we pointed out the significance of the fact that the Gospel of St. Mark begins by introducing the grand figure of John the Baptist, who is contrasted in a marked manner with that of Christ Jesus Himself. If we allow Mark's Gospel to influence us in all its simplicity, we receive a significant impression of John the Baptist; but only when we consider the Baptist against the background of spiritual science does he appear, so to speak, in his full greatness. I have often pointed out that we must interpret the Baptist in the light of the Gospel itself, for we know that he is clearly described in it as a reincarnation of the prophet Elijah (cf. Matt. 11: 14). According to spiritual science, if we wish to investigate the deeper causes of the founding of Christianity and of the Mystery of Golgotha, we must look for the figure of the Baptist against the background of the prophet Elijah. I shall only allude briefly here to the topic of the prophet Elijah since I took advantage of the opportunity provided by the last general meeting of the German section of the Theosophical Society in Berlin to speak more fully on this subject (*Turning Points in Spiritual History*, London, 1934, Lecture 5). All that spiritual science and occult research have to relate concerning the prophet Elijah is fully confirmed by what is contained in the Bible itself. But many passages will undoubtedly remain inexplicable if we read the chapters relating to him in the ordinary way. I will draw your attention only to one point.

We read in the Bible that Elijah challenged all the followers and peoples of King Ahab among whom he lived, and how he pitted himself against his opponents, the priests of Baal, setting up two altars and causing them to lay their sacrifice on one of them while he laid his own sacrifice on the other. He then showed the triviality of what his opponents had said about the priests of Baal because no spiritual greatness was manifested by the god Baal, whereas the greatness and significance of Yahweh or Jehovah appears at once in the case of the sacrifice of Elijah. This was a victory won by Elijah over the followers of Ahab. Then in a remarkable way we are told that Ahab had a neighbor called Naboth who was the owner of a vineyard. Ahab coveted this vineyard, but Naboth would not sell it to him because he regarded it as sacred since it was an inheritance from his father. The Bible then tells us of two facts. On the one side Jezebel, the Queen, was an enemy of Elijah and proclaims that she will have him put to death in the same way as his opponents, the priests of Baal, were put to death because of his victory at the altar. But according to the biblical account, Elijah's death was not brought about through Jezebel. Something else took place. Naboth, the king's neighbor, was summoned to a kind of penitential feast, to which other important persons of the state were also called, and on the occasion of this feast of penitence, he was murdered at the instigation of Jezebel (I Kings 21).

Now we might say that the Bible seems to relate that Naboth was murdered at the urging of Jezebel. Yet Jezebel does not announce that she intends to murder Naboth but rather Elijah. There is an evident discrepancy in the story. Now occult research begins and shows us the real facts in the case, that Elijah was a great spirit who roamed invisibly through the land of Ahab. But at times he entered into and penetrated the soul of Naboth. So Naboth is the physical personality of Elijah; when we speak of the personage of Naboth, we are speaking of the physical personage of Elijah. In the biblical sense, Elijah is the invisible figure, and Naboth his visible image in the physical world. All this I have shown in detail in my lecture entitled, "The Prophet Elijah in the Light of Spiritual Science."*

But if we wish to consider the whole spirit of Elijah's work, and the whole spirit of Elijah as it is presented in the Bible, and allow it to influence our souls, we may say that in Elijah we are confronted by the spirit of the whole ancient Hebrew people. All that lives and is interwoven in this people is encompassed within the spirit of Elijah. We may refer to him as the folk spirit of the ancient Hebrew folk. Spiritual science shows him to have been too great to dwell altogether in the soul of his earthly form, in the soul of Naboth. He hovered over him like a cloud; and he not only lived in Naboth but went around the whole country like an element of nature, active in rain and sunshine. This is revealed ever more clearly the more we go into the whole narrative, which begins by saying that drought and barrenness prevailed, but that through Elijah's relationship to the divine spiritual worlds the drought was ended and the needs of the land at that time were fulfilled. He worked as an element of nature, a law of nature itself. We could say that the best way to learn to recognize what worked in the soul of Elijah is to let the 104th Psalm influence us, with its description of how Yahweh or Jehovah works in all things as a nature-divinity. Of course Elijah is not to be identified with this divinity itself; he is the earthly image of that divinity, an earthly image which is at the same time the folk soul of the Hebrew people. Elijah was a kind of differentiation of Jehovah, an earthly Jehovah, or, as he is described in the Old Testament, the "countenance" of Jehovah.

If we look at it in this way, the fact becomes especially clear that the same spirit that lived in Elijah-Naboth now reappears as John the Baptist. How does he work in John?

---

*Berlin, December 14th, 1911. English translation in *Turning Points in Spiritual History* (London: Rudolf Steiner Publishing Co., 1934).

41

According to the Bible, and especially as is shown in the Gospel of St. Mark, he works through what is called baptism. What in reality is baptism? Why was it administered by John the Baptist to those who allowed themselves to be baptized? Here we must examine what was the actual effect of baptism on those who were baptized. The candidates were immersed in water. Then there always followed what has often been described as happening when a man receives the shock of being threatened by death, for example by falling into the water and nearly drowning, or by nearly falling over a precipice. A loosening of the etheric body takes place; it partly leaves the physical body. As a consequence, something happens that always happens immediately after death, i.e., a kind of retrospect of the past life. That is a well known fact and has often been described even by the materialistic thinkers of the present time. Something similar took place during the baptism by John in the Jordan. The people were plunged into the water. This baptism was not like the usual baptism of today. The baptism of John caused the etheric bodies of the candidates to be loosened and they saw more than they could comprehend with their ordinary powers of understanding. They saw their life in the spirit and the influence of the spirit on this life. They saw also what the Baptist taught, that the old age was fulfilled and that a new age must begin. In the clairvoyant observation that was possible for them for a few seconds during the baptismal immersion they saw that mankind had come to a turning point in evolution, and that what humanity had possessed in former times when it was in a group-soul condition was now in the process of completely dying out; quite new conditions had to come in, and they saw this while in their liberated etheric body. A new impulse, new capacities, must come to humanity. The baptism of John was therefore a question of knowledge. "Transform your minds, but don't merely turn your gaze backwards as would still be possible. Turn your gaze now to something else, to the God who manifests in the human 'I.' The kingdoms of the divine have approached you.'' The Baptist did not only preach that; he made it manifest to them by bestowing the baptism on them in the Jordan. Those who had been baptized knew then as a result of their own clairvoyant observation, even though it lasted but a short time, that the words of the Baptist expressed a world-historical fact.

Only when we consider this connection does the spirit of Elijah, which also worked in John the Baptist, appear to us in the right light. Then we see that Elijah was the spirit of the old Jewish people. What kind of spirit was this? In a certain respect it was already the spirit of the ''I.'' However, it does not appear as the spirit of the individual human being but as the collective folk spirit of the whole people. That which later was to live in each individual man was, so to speak, still in Elijah the group soul of the ancient Hebrew people. That which was to descend as the individual soul into every individual human breast was at the beginning of the Johannine age still in the supersensible world. It was not yet in every human breast, and it could not yet live in this way in Elijah. So it entered into the individual personality of Naboth but only by hovering over it. Yet in Elijah-Naboth it manifested itself more distinctly than it did in the individual members of the ancient Hebrew people. This spirit, hovering, as it were, over man and man's history, was now about to enter more and more into every bosom. This was the great fact now proclaimed by Elijah-John himself when he said, as he baptized the people, something like the following, ''What until now was in the supersensible worlds and worked from these worlds you must now take into your souls as impulses that have come from the kingdom of heaven right into the hearts of men.'' The spirit of Elijah itself shows how in multiplied form it must enter human hearts, so that in the further course of world history they may gradually take up ever more and more of the Christ Impulse. The meaning of the baptism by John was that Elijah was ready to prepare the way for the Christ. This was contained in the deed of the baptism by John in the Jordan, "I will make a place for Him; I will prepare the way for Him into the hearts of men. I will no longer merely hover over men, but will enter into human hearts, so that He also can enter in."

If this is so, what may we then expect? If it is so, there is nothing more natural than to expect something to come to light in John the Baptist that we have already observed in Elijah. It becomes clear how in this grand figure of the Baptist there is not only his individual personality at work, but something more than a personality, which hovers over the individuality like an aura but has an efficacy that transcends it, something alive like an atmosphere among those within whom the Baptist is working. Just as Elijah was active like an atmosphere, so we may expect that as John the Baptist he would again be active like an atmosphere. Indeed, we may expect something further, that this spiritual being of Elijah, now united with John the Baptist, would continue to work on spiritually even if the Baptist were no longer there, if he were away. What does this spiritual being desire? It wishes to prepare the way for the Christ! We can also say that the physical personality of the Baptist may perhaps have left, but his spiritual being like a spiritual atmosphere may remain in the region where he was formerly active, and this spiritual atmosphere actually prepares the very ground on which the Christ could now perform His deed. This is what indeed we might expect. It could perhaps be best expressed if we were to say, "John the Baptist has gone away but what he is as the Elijah-spirit remains, and in this Christ can work best. Here He can best pour forth His words, and in that atmosphere that has remained behind, the Elijah-atmosphere, He can best perform His deeds." That we can expect. And what does Mark's Gospel tell us?

It is very characteristic that twice allusion is made in the Mark Gospel to what I have just indicated. The first time it is said that "immediately after the arrest of John, Jesus came to Galilee and there proclaimed the teaching of the kingdoms of the heavens." (Mark 1: 14.) John therefore was arrested, that is to say, his physical personality was then prevented from working actively. But the figure of Christ Jesus entered into the atmosphere created by him. And it is significant that the same thing occurs a second time in the Mark Gospel, and it is a grandiose fact that it should occur a second time. We must only read the Gospel in the right way. If we pass on to the sixth chapter we hear fully described how King Herod had John the Baptist beheaded. But it is strange how many assumptions were made, not only after the physical personality of John had been arrested, but when he had been removed through death. To some it seemed that the miraculous forces through which Christ Jesus Himself worked were due to the fact that Christ Jesus Himself *was* Elijah, or one of the prophets. But the tortured conscience of Herod arouses a strange foreboding in him. When he hears all that has occurred through Christ Jesus he says, "John, whom I beheaded, has been restored to life!" Herod feels that, though the physical personality of John had gone away, he is now all the more present! He feels that his atmosphere, his spirituality—which was none other than the spirituality of Elijah, is still there. His tormented conscience causes him to be aware that John the Baptist, that is, Elijah, is still there.

But then something strange happens. We are shown how, after John the Baptist had met his physical death, Christ Jesus came to the very neighborhood where John had worked. I want you to take particular notice of a remarkable passage and not to skim over it lightly, for the words of the Gospels are not written for rhetorical effect, nor journalistically. Something very significant is said here. Jesus Christ appears among the throng of followers and disciples of John the Baptist, and this fact is expressed in a sentence to which we must give careful attention: "And as Jesus came out He saw a great crowd," by which could be meant only the disciples of John, "and He had compassion on them . . ." (Mark 6: 34.) Why compassion? Because they had lost their master, they were there without John, whose headless corpse we are told had been carried to his grave. But even more precisely is it said, "for they were like sheep who had lost their shepherd. And He began to teach them many things." It cannot be indicated any more clearly how He teaches John's disciples. He teaches them because the spirit of Elijah, which is at the same time the spirit of John the Baptist, is still active among them. Thus it is again indicated with dramatic power in these significant passages of the Mark Gospel how the spirit of Christ Jesus entered into what had been prepared by the spirit of Elijah-John. Even so this is only one of the main points, around which many other significant things are grouped.

I will now call your attention to one thing more. I have several times pointed out how this spirit of Elijah or John continued to act in such a way as to impress its impulses into world history. And since we are all anthroposophists assembled together here, and able to enter into occult facts, it is permissible to discuss this subject here. I have often mentioned that the soul of Elijah-John appeared again in the painter Raphael. This is one of those facts that call attention to the metamorphoses of souls that take place under the impetus given by the Mystery of Golgotha. Because it was also necessary that in the post-Christian era such a soul should work in Raphael through the medium of a single personality; what in ancient times was so comprehensive and world encompassing now appears in such a different personality as that of Raphael. Can we not feel that the aura that hovered round Elijah-John is also present in Raphael? That in Raphael there were such similarities to these two others that we could even say that this element was too great to be able to enter into a single personality but hovered round it, so that the revelations received by this personality seemed like an illumination? Such was indeed the case with Raphael!

I could also say that there exists a proof of this fact, though it is a somewhat personal one, to which I already alluded in Munich. I should like to refer to it again here, not for the purpose of bringing out the personality of John the Baptist, but the full being of Elijah-John. For this purpose I will venture to speak of the further progress of the soul of Elijah-John in Raphael. Anyone who wishes honestly and sincerely to investigate what Raphael really was is likely to have his feelings aroused in a very remarkable way.

I have drawn attention to the modern art historian Hermann Grimm, and have mentioned that he was able to produce a biography of Michelangelo with comparative facility, but that on three separate occasions he tried to prepare a kind of life of Raphael. And because Hermann Grimm was not a so-called "learned man"—such a man of course can do anything he sets out to do—but a universal man who threw his whole heart sincerely into whatever he wanted to investigate and understand, he was forced to admit that when he had finished what he had intended to be a life of Raphael it did not turn out to be a life of Raphael at all. So he had to begin to do it again and again, but he was never satisfied with his work. Shortly before his death he made one more attempt, which is included in his posthumous works. In this he tried to approach Raphael and understand him in the way his heart wished to understand him, and the title his new work was to bear was indeed characteristic of him. He proposed to call the book *Raphael as World-Power*. For it seemed to him that if one approaches Raphael honestly, he cannot be described in any way other than as a world-power, unless one fails to see through to what is actively at work in world history. It is very natural that a modern author should experience some discomfort in choosing his words if he is to write as freely and frankly as did the evangelists. Even the best writers of modern times are embarrassed if they set to work in this way, but the figures that have to be described often force them to use the appropriate words. So it is very remarkable how Hermann Grimm wrote about Raphael shortly before his death in the first chapters of his book. It is really as if one can sense in the heart of Hermann Grimm something of the circumstances surrounding such a figure as that of Elijah-John, when he said, "If by some miracle Michelangelo were called back from the dead to live among us, and I were to meet him, I would respectfully stand aside to let him pass by. But if Raphael were to come my way I would go up behind him to see if by chance I might hear a few words from his lips. In the case of Leonardo and Michelangelo we can confine ourselves to relating what they once were in their own time; but with Raphael one must begin with what he is to us today. A slight veil has been cast over the others, but not over Raphael. He belongs among those whose growth will continue for a long time yet. We may imagine that Raphael will present ever new riddles to future generations of humanity." (*Fragments*, Vol. II, page 170.)

Hermann Grimm describes Raphael as a world-power, as a spirit striding on through centuries and millennia, as a spirit who could not be encompassed within one individual man. And we may read yet other words by Hermann Grimm, wrung from the honesty and sincerity of his soul. It seems as if he wanted to express that there is something about Raphael like a great aura enveloping him, just as the spirit of Elijah enveloped Naboth. Could this be expressed in any other way than in these words of Hermann Grimm, "Raphael is a citizen of world-history; he is like one of the four rivers which, according to the belief of the ancient world, flowed out of Paradise." (*Fragments*, Vol. II, page 153.)

That might also have been written by an evangelist, and it might almost have been written of Elijah! Thus even a modern historian of art, if his feelings are honest and sincere, is able to feel something of the great cosmic impulses that live through the ages. Truly nothing further is required to understand spiritual science than to come close to the soul and spiritual needs of those men who strive longingly to discover the truth about the evolution of humanity.

So does John the Baptist stand before us, and it is good if we can feel him in this way when we read the opening words of the Mark Gospel, and again later in the sixth chapter. The Bible is unlike a book of modern scholarship in which it is clearly emphasized what people ought to read. The Bible conceals beneath the grandiose artistic and occult style many of the mysterious facts it wishes to proclaim. And it is precisely in relation to the facts in the story of John the Baptist that the artistic and occult style does indeed conceal such things. Here I want to draw your attention to something that you can perhaps experience as truth only through your life of feeling. If you admit that there can be truths other than rational ones you may be able to see that the Bible tells us how the spirit or soul of Elijah is related to the spirit or soul of John the Baptist. Let us as briefly as we can see how far this is the case by allowing ourselves to be affected by the description of Elijah as it appears in the Old Testament:

> So Elijah arose and went toward Zaraphta. And when he came to the gate of the city, there was a widow woman gathering wood. And he called to her and said "Bring me, I pray thee, a little water in a pitcher that I may drink." And as she was going to fetch it, he called out to her and said "Bring me also a mouthful of bread."
>
> And the woman said, "As sure as the Lord your God liveth I have no bread, only a handful of flour in a bin and a little oil in a cruse. And see, I have gathered a few pieces of

49

wood, and I am about to go inside and I want to make them ready for me and my son that we may eat and then die.''

Elijah said to her, ''Fear not, go in and do as you have said. But first make a small cake and bring it out for me. Then afterwards you can make something for you and your son. For thus says the Lord, 'The flour in the bin shall not be consumed nor the oil cruse run dry until the day when the Lord makes it rain upon the earth.' ''

So she went in and did as Elijah had said. And he ate, and so did her household for a time. The flour in the bin was not eaten up, and the oil cruse did not run dry, according to the word he had spoken through Elijah. (I Kings 17: 10–16.)

What do we read in the story of Elijah? We read of the coming of Elijah to a widow, and of a marvellous increase of bread. Because the spirit of Elijah was there it came about that there was no want in spite of the shortage of bread. The bread increased—so we read—the moment Elijah came into the presence of the widow. What is described here as an increase in bread, as the giving of bread as a gift, comes about through the spirit of Elijah. We can say therefore that the fact shines out from the Old Testament that the increase of bread is effected through the appearance of Elijah.

Now let us turn to the sixth chapter of the Mark Gospel. Here we are told how Herod caused John to be beheaded, and how Christ Jesus then came to the group of John's followers.

And when He came out He saw a great crowd, and had compassion on them, for they were like sheep without a shepherd. And He began to teach them many things. And as it had become quite late His disciples came to Him and said, ''This is a desolate place and it is already late. Let them go so that they may go to the farms and villages and buy themselves something to eat.'' But He answered them, ''You give them something to eat.'' And they said to Him,

"Should we go there and buy bread for two hundred denarii and give them something to eat?" He answered them, "How many loaves do you have? Go and look." And after they had obtained the information they said, "Five loaves and two fishes."

And he ordered them all to sit down on the green grass as if it had been a table. And they lay down as if for bed, by hundreds and by fifties. And he took the five loaves and the two fishes, looked up to heaven, blessed and broke the loaves and gave them to the disciples to set before them; in the same way he divided the two fishes among them. And they all ate and were satisfied. (Mark 6: 34–42.)

You know the story; again there was an increase in bread brought about by the spirit of Elijah-John. The Bible does not actually speak "clearly" as we understand the word today, but it expresses what it has to say through its composition. Whoever understands how to value the truths of feeling will wish to let his feeling dwell on the passage where it is related how Elijah came to the widow and increased the bread, and where the reincarnated Elijah leaves his physical body and Christ Jesus brings about in a new form what is described as an increase of bread. Such are the inner developments, the inner correspondences in the Bible. They demonstrate how fundamentally empty the scholarship is that talks about a "compilation of biblical fragments," but also how it is possible for us to recognize the one single spirit composing it throughout, irrespective of who this single spirit is. That is how the Baptist is presented to us.

Now it is very remarkable how the Baptist himself is again introduced into the work of Christ Jesus. On two occasions it is indicated to us that Christ Jesus really entered the aura of the Baptist just when the physical personage was withdrawing more and more into the background, finally leaving the physical plane altogether. But it is shown in very clear words precisely through the very simplicity of the Mark Gospel how through the entry of Christ Jesus into the element of Elijah-John a wholly new impulse enters the world. In order to understand this we must envisage the whole description given in the Gospel from the moment when Christ Jesus appears after the arrest of John the Baptist and speaks of the divine kingdom, to the passage where the murder of John by Herod is related, and continue on with the subsequent chapters. If we take all these stories down to the story of Herod and consider them in their true character we find that the intention of all of them is to reveal in a correct manner the qualities that are characteristic of Christ Jesus. Yesterday we spoke of His characteristic way of acting so that He is recognized also by the spirits which live in those possessed by demons. In other words, He is recognized by supersensible beings and this is presented to us in a sharply accentuated manner. And then we are faced with the fact that that which lives in Christ Jesus is something in reality quite different from what dwelt in Elijah-Naboth for the reason that the spirit of Elijah could not wholly enter into Naboth.

The purpose of the Gospel of St. Mark is to show us that the being of Christ entered fully into Jesus of Nazareth and entirely filled his earthly personality. What we recognize as the universal human ego was working in Him. What then is so terrible to the demons who were in possession of human beings when they were confronted by Christ Jesus? The devils are compelled to say to Him, "You are He who bears the God within You." They recognize Him as a divine power in the human personality, thus compelling the demons to allow themselves to be recognized and to come forth from the human beings who were possessed through the power of what lives in the individual personality of man (Mark 1: 24; 3: 11; 5: 7). This is why in the early chapters of the Mark Gospel the figure of Christ is worked out so carefully, making Him in a certain way a contrast to Elijah-Naboth, and also to Elijah-John. For whereas that which was active in them could not wholly live in them, this activating quality was wholly contained within Christ Jesus. For this reason, although a cosmic principle lives in Him, Christ Jesus as an individual personality confronts other human beings quite individually, including those whom He heals.

It is true that at the present time people generally take descriptions that come from the past in a peculiar way. In particular many of the modern learned students of nature—monists, as they also call themselves—take these descriptions in a very peculiar way when they wish to present their conceptions of the world. We could characterize this attitude by saying that these learned savants and excellent natural philosophers are secretly of the opinion, though they might be too embarrassed to say so, that it would have been better if the Lord God had left the organizing of the world to them, for they would really have established it better.

Take, for example, the case of such a learned student of natural philosophy of our time who maintains that wisdom has come to mankind only in the last twenty years, while others believe it has only been during the last five years, and regard earlier ideas as mere superstition. Such a man would profoundly regret that at the time of Christ there was no modern school of scientific medicine with its various remedies. According to their notions it would have been much more clever if all these people, for example Simon Peter's mother-in-law and others, had been cured with the aid of modern medical remedies. To their minds he would have been a really perfect God if he had created the world in accordance with the conceptions of a modern knowledge of nature. He would not have allowed humanity to have been deprived so long of the knowledge of nature possessed by modern savants. The world as established by God is indeed bungled by comparison with what a modern natural scientist would have created. They are embarrassed to say it so openly, but it is possible to read between the lines. These things that whirr around in the minds of materialistic natural scientists should be called by their right names. If we could for once talk confidentially with one of these gentlemen we might hear him voice the opinion that it is hard to avoid being an atheist when one sees how little success God had at the time of Christ in curing human beings by the methods of modern natural science.

But one thing is not considered: that the word "evolution," about which people speak so often, ought to be taken seriously and honestly. Everything about evolution must be understood if the world is to reach its goal, and it is pointless to go looking for a plan such as modern natural scientists would produce if they were able to create a world. Because they think in this way, men do not correctly realize that the whole constitution of man, the unity of the finer bodies of man, were formerly quite different. In earlier times nothing at all could have been achieved with the human personality through the methods of natural science. For then the etheric body was much more active, much stronger than it is today; hence the physical body could be worked on indirectly through the etheric body in a very different manner. To express it quite dryly, at that time there was quite a different effect when one healed by means of "feeling" from what it would be today. At that time feeling was poured out from one person into another. When the etheric body was really much stronger and still governed the physical body, psycho-spiritual methods of healing acted quite differently. Human beings were constitutionally different, so there had to be a different method for healing. If a natural scientist does not know this he will say, "We no longer believe in miracles, and what is said here about healing is really a question of miracles, and these we must leave out of consideration."

And if one is a modern enlightened theologian one is faced by a very special dilemma. He would like to be able to retain these ideas, but at the same time he is filled with the modern prejudice that there is no such thing as healing of this kind, and that such cures are necessarily miracles. Which leads on to the effort to make all kinds of explanations as to the possibility or impossibility of miracles. But one thing he does not know. Nothing described up to the sixth chapter of the Mark Gospel was at that time regarded as a miracle, any more than when today some function of the human organization is affected by one medicament or another. No one at that time would have thought of it as a miracle if someone stretched out his hand and said to a leper, "I will it, become clean." The whole natural being of Christ Jesus that was poured forth here, was in itself the cure. It would no longer work today because the union between the physical and etheric body is quite different. In those days physicians usually healed in that way, so it was not something that should be particularly emphasized that Christ Jesus cured lepers through compassion and the laying on of hands. Such a thing was then a matter of course. What is worthy of note in this chapter is something quite different, and this we must picture to ourselves correctly.

Let us then first glance at the manner in which the great physicians and even the lesser ones were trained. They were trained in schools that were part of the mystery schools, and they were able to attain to powers that worked down through them from the supersensible world. Such physicians were thus in a sense mediums for the transmission of supersensible powers. Through their own mediumship these men transmitted supersensible powers, and they had been trained for this in the medical mystery schools. When in this way a physician laid his hands on a person it was not his own powers that streamed down but powers from the supersensible world. It was through his initiation in the mystery schools that he could become a channel for the working of supersensible powers. It would not have seemed especially remarkable to a person of that time if he heard that a leper or someone suffering from a fever had been cured through such psychical processes. The significant aspect was not that someone appeared capable of curing in this way but that someone who had not been trained in a mystery school could heal in this manner, and that in the heart and soul of this man the power which earlier flowed from the higher worlds was present, and such powers had now become personal individual powers. The truth was to be made clear that the time was fulfilled, and that from now onward men were no longer to be channels for supersensible forces, that this had come to an end. This had also become clear to those who had been baptized by John in the Jordan, that the old time was coming to an end and everything in the future must be done through the human "I," through that which is to enter into the divine inner center of the human being. They recognized that now among the people there stands one who does out of His own self what others before had done with the help of beings who live in the supersensible world and whose powers worked down on them.

So we by no means grasp the meaning of the Bible if we picture to ourselves the curative process as being something special. In the fading light of the era that was passing away, when such cures were possible, it is said that Christ performed cures during this era of the fading light, but that He healed with new forces which would be present from that time onward. Thus it is very clearly shown, with a clarity that cannot be obscured, that Christ Jesus works entirely from man to man. This is everywhere emphasized. It could scarcely be more clearly expressed than when Jesus comes in contact with a woman described in the fifth chapter of the Mark Gospel. He heals her because she approaches Him and touches His garment, and He feels that a current of

56

force has gone out from Him. The whole story is related in such a way as to show that the woman draws near to Christ Jesus and takes hold of His garment. At first He does nothing else Himself, but *she* does something; she takes hold of His garment, whereupon a current of force leaves Him. How? Not in this instance because He has released it, but because she draws it forth, and He notices it only later. This is very clearly shown. And when He does notice it what does He say? "Daughter, your faith has aided you. Go in peace and be healed from your plague."

He only then became aware Himself, as He stood there, how the divine kingdom was streaming into Him, and streamed out from Him again. He does not stand there before those who are to be cured as the healers of earlier times stood before those from whom they were to drive out their demons. Whether the sick person believed or did not believe, the power that streamed from the supersensible worlds through the medium of the healer streamed into him. But now, when it depended on the ego, this ego had to participate in the process; everything now became individualized. The main point of this description was not that one could influence the body through the soul—in that epoch that would have been a matter of course—but that insofar as the new age was just beginning, one ego must henceforth be in direct relationship with another ego. In earlier times the spiritual lived in the higher worlds, and it hovered over the human being. Now the kingdoms of heaven came near and were to enter into the hearts of men, were to live within the hearts of men as in a center. That is the point. In a world view such as this the outer physical and the inner moral flowed together in a new way, in such a way that from the time of the founding of Christianity until today there could only be faith, which from now onward can become knowledge.

Let us take the case of a sick person in ancient times as he stood facing his physician who was to heal him in the way

I have just described. Magical forces were brought down from the spiritual worlds through the medium of the physician who had been prepared for this in the mystery schools, and these forces streamed through the body of the physician into that of the patient. There was at that time no link with the moral element, for the whole process did not affect the ego. Morality had nothing to do with it, for the forces flowed down magically from the higher worlds. Now a new era begins, and the moral and the physical aspects of the healing worked together in a new way. Knowledge of this fact will enable us to understand another story.

> Some days had passed when He came again to Capernaum. When it was reported that He was in the house many people gathered there, so that there was no longer any room for them, even in front of the door, and He preached the word to them. Then they came to Him with a paralytic carried by four men. And when they were unable to come close to Him because of the crowd, they removed the roof of the house where He was and let down the litter on which the paralytic was lying through the gap. And when Jesus saw their faith, He said to the paralytic, "Son, your sins are forgiven you." (Mark 2: 1-5.)

What would a physician have said in earlier times? What would the scribes and Pharisees have expected when a healing was to take place? They would have expected such a healer to have said, "The forces now pouring into you and into your paralyzed limbs will enable you to move." But what did Christ say? "Your sins are forgiven you." That is the moral element in which the ego participates. It was a language the Pharisees were incapable of understanding. They could not understand it; for someone to speak like this was a blasphemy to the Pharisees. Why? Because to their minds God could be spoken of only as living in the supersensible worlds, and He works down from there; and sins could be forgiven only from the supersensible worlds. They could not understand that forgiveness of sins had something to do with the person who healed. Therefore Christ went on further to say: "Which is it easier to say to the paralytic, 'Your sins are forgiven,' or 'Stand up, take up your litter and walk?' But so that you may know that the Son of Man has authority to forgive sins on earth" (turning to the paralytic) "I tell you to stand up, take up your litter and go home." And at once he stood up, took his litter and went out in full view of everyone. (Mark 2: 9–12.)

Christ combines the moral and magical elements in His healing, and in this way made the transition from the ego-less to the ego-filled condition, and this can be found in every single description. This is how these matters must be understood, for this is the way they are told. Now compare what spiritual science has to say with all that biblical commentaries have to say about the "forgiveness of sins." You will find there the strangest explanations, but nowhere anything satisfying because it was not known what the Mystery of Golgotha actually was.

I said that it had to be taken on faith. Why on faith? Because the expression of the moral in the physical element is not developed in one incarnation. When we meet someone today we must not look upon a physical defect as the bringing together of the physical and moral elements within one incarnation. Only when we go beyond one individual incarnation do we find the connection between the moral and physical elements in his *karma*. Because karma was very little emphasized up to the present time or not at all we can now say, "Until now the connection between the moral and physical elements could be discerned only through faith. But now, when we are approaching the Gospels in a spiritual scientific way, faith is replaced by knowledge. Christ Jesus stands here beside us as an enlightened one, telling us about karma, when He makes known, "This person I may cure, for I perceived from his personality that his karma is such that he may stand up and walk."

In such a passage as this you can see how the Bible is to be understood only if it is provided with the means given by modern spiritual science. It is our task to show that in this book, this cosmic book, the profoundest wisdom concerning the evolution of man is truly embodied. Once we are able to grasp what cosmic processes unfold on the earth—and this we shall emphasize increasingly in the course of these particular lectures since the Mark Gospel especially points to them—then we shall discover that what can be said in connection with this Gospel in the future can in no way be offensive to any other of the world's creeds. True knowledge of the Bible will, because of its own inner strength, stand firmly on the ground of spiritual science, attaching equal value to all the religious creeds of the world. This is because true knowledge of the Bible, for the reasons given at the end of our last lecture, cannot be truthfully confined within one denomination or another, but must be universal. In this way the religions will be reconciled. What I was able to tell you in my first lecture about the Indian who gave the lecture, "Christ and Christianity," seems like the beginning of such a reconciliation. This Indian, no doubt subject to all the prejudices of his nation, nevertheless looked up to Christ in an interdenominational sense. It will be the task of spiritual scientific activity within the different religious confessions to try to understand this figure of Christ. For it seems to me that the task of our spiritual movement must be to deepen the religious creeds so that the inner nature of the different religions can be understood and deepened.

I should like in this connection to indicate something I have often pictured for you in the past, e.g., how a Buddhist who is an anthroposophist would conduct himself in relation to an anthroposophist who is a Christian. The Buddhist would say, "Gautama Buddha, who after first being a Bodhisattva then became a Buddha, after his death reached such a height that he no longer needs to return to earth."

The Christian who is an anthroposophist would reply, "I understand, for if I find my way into your heart and believe what you believe, I myself believe that about your Buddha." This is what it means to understand the religion of the other person, to bring oneself to the other's religion. The Christian who has become an anthroposophist can understand everything that the other man says.

And what would the Buddhist who has become an anthroposophist say in reply? He would say, "I am trying to grasp what the innermost core of Christianity is. That with Christ we do not have to do with a founder of religion but with something different. In the case of the Mystery of Golgotha we have to do with an impersonal fact. Jesus of Nazareth did not stand there as the founder of a new religion, but the Christ entered into him, and He died on the Cross, thus accomplishing the Mystery of Golgotha. What is really the issue is that the Mystery of Golgotha is a cosmic fact." And the Buddhist will say, "In future I shall no longer misunderstand, now that I have grasped the essence of your religion, as you have grasped mine, which was the issue between us. I will never picture the Christ as someone who will be reincarnated. For you the central question is what happened there. And I should be speaking in a very odd manner if I were to say that Christianity could be improved upon in any respect—that if Christ Jesus had been better understood He would not have been crucified after three years, that a religious founder should have been treated differently, and the like. The point is precisely that Christ was crucified, and the crucial consequences of that death on the Cross. There is no point in thinking that an injustice occurred at that time and that Christianity today could be improved upon." No Buddhist who is an anthroposophist could say anything else than, "As you truly strive to understand the essence of my religion, so will I truly strive to understand the essence of yours."

61

And what would be the result if people of different religions were to understand each other in such a way that the Christian were to say to the Buddhist, "I believe in your Buddha just as you do," and if the Buddhist were to say to the Christian, "I understand the Mystery of Golgotha in the same way you do?" If something like this were to become general among human beings, what would be the consequence? There would be peace, and mutual acceptance of all religions among men. And this must come. The anthroposophical movement must consist of a true mutual understanding of all religions. It would be contrary to the spirit of anthroposophy if a Christian who became an anthroposophist were to say to a Buddhist, "It is untrue that Gautama after he became a Buddha will no longer reincarnate. He must appear in the twentieth century again as a physical human being." Whereupon the Buddhist would say, "Can your anthroposophy lead you only to deride my religion?" And as a result instead of peace discord would arise among the religions. In the same way a Christian would have to tell a Buddhist who insisted on speaking about the possible improvements in Christianity, "If you can maintain that the Mystery of Golgotha was a mistake, and that Christ could return in a physical body so that He could succeed better than before, then you are making no effort to understand my religion, you are deriding it." It is no task of anthroposophy to deride any religion, old or new, that is worthy of respect. If this were the task of anthroposophy it would be founding a society on mutual derision, not on the understanding of the equality of all religions!

In order to understand the spirit and the occult core of anthroposophy we must write this in our souls. And we can do this in no better way than by extending the strength and love that are working in the Gospels to the understanding of all religions. The later lectures in this cycle will show us how this can be achieved most particularly in connection with the Gospel of St. Mark.

LECTURE 4

Today I should like first of all to call your attention to and place before your mind's eye two pictures drawn from the evolution of man during the last few thousand years. I shall first direct your attention to something that occurred about the middle and toward the end of the fifth century B.C. It is well known to all of you, but, as I said, we shall look back at it with the eyes of our soul.

We see how the Buddha had gathered a number of disciples and pupils around him in the land of India, and how, from what took place then between the Buddha and his disciples and pupils, there arose the great and mighty movement that began and flowed on for centuries in the East, throwing up mighty waves and bringing to countless people inner salvation, inner freedom of soul, and an uplifting of human consciousness. If we wish to characterize what happened at that time we need only envisage the main content of Buddha's teachings and actions.

Life as it is lived by man in his earthly incarnations is suffering because through the sequence of his incarnations he is always subject to the urge for ever new incarnations. To free oneself from this yearning for reincarnation is a goal worth striving for. This goal is to blot out of the soul everything that can call forth the desire for physical incarnation, with the aim of at last ascending to an existence in which the soul no longer feels the desire to be connected with life through the physical senses and physical organs, but to ascend and take part in what is called *Nirvana*. This is the great teaching that flowed from the lips of the Buddha, that life means suffering and that man must find a means to free himself from suffering so as to be able to share in Nirvana. If we wish to picture to ourselves in precise but familiar con-

63

cepts the impulse contained in the wonderful teaching of Buddha, we could perhaps say that the Buddha directed the minds of his pupils through the strength and power of his individuality to earth existence; while at the same time through the infinite fullness of his compassion he tried also to give them the means to raise their souls and all that was within them from the earthly to the heavenly, to raise human thinking and human philosophy from the human to the divine.

We might picture this as a formula if we wish to characterize clearly and correctly the impulse that went out from the great sermon of the Buddha at Benares. We see the Buddha gathering around him his faithful pupils. What do we perceive in the souls of these disciples? What will they eventually come to believe? That all the striving of the human soul must be directed toward becoming free from the yearning for rebirth, free from the inclination toward sense existence, free to seek the perfecting of the self by freeing it from everything that binds it to sense existence, and connecting it with all that links it to its divine spiritual origin. Such were the feelings that lived in the disciples of the Buddha. They sought to free themselves from all the temptations of life and let their only link with the world be the perception of the soul shining into the spiritual that is experienced in compassion; to become absorbed in striving for spiritual perfection, free from all earthly wants, with the aim of having as little as possible to do with what binds the external man to earthly existence. In this mood the pupils of the Buddha wandered through the world, and it was in this manner that they glimpsed the aims and objectives of Buddhist discipleship.

And if we follow up the centuries during which Buddhism was spreading and ask ourselves what lived in the hearts and souls of the Buddha's adherents and what it was that lived in the dissemination of Buddhism, we receive the answer that these men were devoted to lofty aims, but in the midst of all their thinking, feeling, and perception the great figure of the Buddha was living, together with everything that he had said in such thrilling, significant words about the deliverance from the sorrow of life. In the midst of all their thinking and perception, the comprehensive, all-encompassing, mighty authority of the Buddha lived in the hearts of his pupils and successors down the centuries. Everything the Buddha had said was looked upon by these pupils and succesors as holy writ.

Why was it that the words of the Buddha sounded like a message from heaven to his pupils and successors? It was because these pupils and successors lived in the faith and belief that during the event of the Bodhi-tree the true knowledge of cosmic existence had flashed up in the soul of the Buddha, and the light and sun of the universe shone into it, with the consequence that everything that flowed from his lips had to be thought of as if it was the utterance of the spirits of the universe. It was this mood as it lived in the hearts of the pupils and successors of the Buddha, the holiness and uniqueness of this mood that was all-important. We wish to place all this before our spiritual eye so that we may learn to understand what happened there half a millennium before the Mystery of Golgotha.

Now we turn our gaze to another picture from world history. For in the long ages of human evolution what is separated by about a century may really be considered contemporary. In the thousands and thousands of years of human evolution a single century is of little importance. Therefore we can say that if the picture we wish to place before our souls is historically to be put a century later, as far as human evolution is concerned it was almost contemporary with the event of Buddha that we have just described.

In the fifth century B.C. we see another individuality gradually gathering pupils and adherents around himself in ancient Greece. Again this fact is well known. But if we are to come to an understanding of the last centuries it is a good thing to picture this individuality in our minds. We see Socrates in ancient Greece gathering pupils around himself, and indeed we need to mention Socrates in this connection even if we only consider the picture drawn of Socrates by the great philosopher Plato, a picture which in its essentials seems to be confirmed by the great philosopher Aristotle. If we consider the striking picture of Socrates as presented by Plato, then we can also say that a movement began with Socrates that then spread into the West. Anyone who visualizes the whole character of Western cultural development is bound to conclude that the Socratic element was a determining factor for everything in the West. Although the Socratic element in the West spreads through the waves of world history more subtly than the Buddhistic element in the East, we are still entitled to draw a parallel between Socrates and the Buddha. But we must certainly make a clear differentiation between the pupils and disciples of Socrates and the pupils and disciples of the Buddha. When we consider the fundamental difference between the Buddha and Socrates we may indeed say that we are confronted with everything that differentiates the East from the West.

Socrates gathers his pupils around himself, but how does he feel in relation to them? His manner of treating these pupils has been called the art of a spiritual midwife because he wished to draw out from the souls of his pupils what they themselves knew, and what they were to learn. He put his questions in such a manner that the fundamental inner mood of the souls of his pupils was stirred to movement. He transmitted nothing from himself to his pupils, but elicited everything from them. The somewhat dry and prosaic aspect of Socrates' view of the world and the way he presented it comes from the fact that Socrates actually appealed to the independence and to the innate reasoning power of every pupil. Though he wandered through the streets of Athens in a rather different way from the way the Buddha walked with his pupils, there is nevertheless a similarity. On the one hand the Buddha revealed to his pupils what he had received through his enlightenment under the Bodhi tree, and by allowing what he had thus received from the spiritual world to stream down to his pupils he enabled what had lived in him to live on in his pupils and remain active for centuries. On the other hand, Socrates did not make the slightest claim to go on living as Socrates in the hearts of his pupils. When he was talking with his pupils Socrates did not wish to transmit anything at all of himself into their souls. He wished to leave it to them to draw out from themselves what they already possessed. Nothing of Socrates was to pass over into his pupils' souls, nothing at all.

We can think of no greater contrast than that between the Buddha and Socrates. The Buddha was to live on in the souls of his pupils, whereas in the souls of the pupils of Socrates nothing more was to live on than what the midwife has given to the child who comes into the world. Thus the spiritual element in the pupils of Socrates was to be drawn forth by the spiritual midwifery of Socrates when he left each person on his own, drawing forth from each one of them what was already there within him. That was the intention of Socrates. So we could characterize the difference between Socrates and the Buddha in the following way. If a voice from heaven had wished to state clearly what the disciples of Buddha were to receive through the Buddha, it might well have said, "Kindle within yourselves what lived in the Buddha, so that through him you can find the path to existence in the spirit." If we wish to characterize in the same way what Socrates wanted we should have to say, "Become what you are!"

If we bring these two pictures before our souls, ought we not to say to ourselves that we are here confronted with two different streams of development in human evolution, and that they are polar opposites? They do meet again in a certain way, but only in the farthest distance. We should not mix these things together but rather characterize them in their differentiation, and only then indicate that there is at the same time a higher unity. If we think of the Buddha face to face with one of his pupils we could say that he is trying to kindle in the souls of his disciples what is necessary to lead them upward to the spiritual worlds through what he himself had experienced under the Bodhi tree. This may be recognized in the form of his discourses, with their sublime words and their endless repetitions, repetitions that should not be omitted in translation. The words are chosen in such a way that they sound like a heavenly proclamation from the heavenly world coming from beyond the earth, spoken through his lips out of the direct experience of what had happened during his enlightenment, words which he wished to pass on to his followers.

How then can we picture Socrates with his pupils? They confront each other in such a way that when Socrates is trying to make clear to his pupils the relation of man to the divine using the simplest rational considerations of everyday life, he shows them the logical connection between these considerations. The pupil is always directed to the most prosaic everyday matters, and his task is then to apply ordinary logic to what he has grasped as knowledge. Only once is Socrates shown as having risen to the height at which he could, as we might say, speak as Buddha spoke to his pupils. Only once does he appear like this, and that is at the moment when he was approaching death. When just before his death he spoke about the immortality of the soul he was surely speaking then like one of the highest of the enlightened ones. Yet at the same time what he said could only be understood if one takes into account his entire life experience. It is for this reason that what he said then touches our

68

heart and soul when we listen to his Platonic discourse on immortality in which he speaks somewhat as follows, "Have I not striven all my life to attain through philosophy all that a man can in order to become free from the world of sense? Now when my soul is soon to be released from everything material, ought it not to penetrate joyfully into the world of spirit? Should I not be ready to penetrate with joy into that for which I have inwardly striven through philosophy?"

Anyone who can grasp the whole mood of this dialogue of Socrates in the *Phaedo* finds himself experiencing a feeling similar to that experienced by the pupils of the Buddha when they listened to his sublime teachings, so that it is possible to say that in spite of the difference, the polar difference between these two individualities, at a particular moment they are so sublime that even in this polar difference a certain unity appears. If we direct our vision to the Buddha we shall find that the discourses of Buddha as a whole are such that they arouse a feeling which one has with Socrates only in the case of the discourse on the immortality of the soul. I am referring to the soul-mood, the spiritual tension of this dialogue. But what is poured forth in the other discourses of Socrates which are always directed to a man's own reason is not often met with in the Buddha, although it is occasionally to be found. It sometimes sounds through. One can actually experience it as a kind of metamorphosed Socratic dialogue when on one occasion the Buddha wishes to make clear to his pupil Sona that it is not good to stay only in the realm of the material and enmeshed in sense-existence, nor yet to mortify the flesh and live like the old aescetics. It is good to pursue a middle path. Here the Buddha confronts his pupil Sona and speaks to him somewhat in the following manner, "See here, Sona, would you be able to play well on a lute whose strings are too loose?" "No," Sona is forced to reply, "I shall not be able to play well on a lute whose strings are too loose." "Well, then, will you be able to play well on a lute whose strings are too tight?'' ''No,'' Sona must answer, ''I shall not be able to play well on a lute whose strings are drawn too tight.'' ''When will you be able to play well on the lute?'' Buddha then asks him. ''When the strings are drawn neither too loosely nor too tightly.'' ''So it is also with man,'' rejoined the Buddha. ''If he is too much attached to the life of the senses he cannot wholly listen to the voice of reason. Nor will he truly listen to reason if he spends his life mortifying himself and withdrawing from earthly life. The middle path which must be taken also when stringing the lute must likewise be followed in relation to the mood of the human soul.''

This is just the way Socrates talks to his pupils, making an appeal to their reason, so that this dialogue of the Buddha with his pupil could equally well have been devised by Socrates. What I have given you is a ''Socratic dialogue'' carried on by the Buddha with his pupil Sona. But in just the same way that the discourse of Socrates to his pupils just before his death, a discourse that I have called Buddhistic, was unusual for Socrates, so is a dialogue of this kind rare in the case of the Buddha. We must never fail to emphasize the fact that we can reach the truth only by making characterizations of this kind. It would be easier to make a characterization if we were to say something along these lines, ''It is through great leaders that humanity moves forward. What these leaders say is essentially the same thing though it takes different forms. All the individual leaders of mankind proclaim in their teachings different aspects of the same truth.'' Such a statement is of course quite true, but it could scarcely be more trivial. What is important is that we should take the trouble to recognize things in such a way that we look for both the differentiations and the underlying unity; that we should characterize things according to their differences, and only afterward look for the higher unity to be perceived in these differences.

I felt that this remark about method was one that I had to make because in spiritual studies it usually is in accord with reality. It would be so easy to say that all religions contain the same thing and then concentrate on this one thing and then characterize it by saying, "All the various religious founders have presented only the same one thing in different forms." But if we do make this characterization, it will remain infinitely trivial, however beautiful the words in which we express it. It would be just as unproductive as if we wished from the beginning to characterize two such figures as the Buddha and Socrates in the light of some abstract unity without seeking to perceive the polar difference between them. But if we trace them back to their forms of thought the matter will quickly be understood. Pepper and salt, sugar and paprika, are all put on the table to add to the food—they are all one, that is to say they are condiments. But because this can be said of them it does not mean that we must say all these condiments are the same and sugar our coffee by adding salt or pepper to it. What is unacceptable in life should not be accepted in spiritual matters. It would be unacceptable to say that Krishna and Zarathustra, Orpheus and Hermes are fundamentally only variations of the "one thing." It is no more useful to make a characterization like this than it would be to say that pepper and salt, sugar and paprika are all different variations of one essence, since they are all equally condiments for food. It is important that we should grasp this point about method, and that we should not accept what is comfortable in preference to the truth.

If we visualize these two figures, the Buddha and Socrates, they will seem to us like two different, polar opposite configurations of the evolutionary streams of mankind. And when we now link these two within a higher unity as we have done, we may add to them a third in whom we also have to do with a great individuality around whom gather pupils and disciples—Christ Jesus. If among those pupils and disciples who gather around Him we fix our attention first on the Twelve, then we find that the Gospel of Mark in particular tells us with the utmost clarity something about the relation of the master to his pupils, in the same way as we characterized the relation with the greatest clarity we could between Buddha and Socrates in a different domain. And what was the clearest, the most striking and concise expression of this relationship? It is when the Christ—and this is indicated on several occasions—faced the crowd that wished to hear Him. He speaks to this crowd in parables and imagery. And the Gospel of Mark pictures this in a simple and grandiose manner when it describes how certain profound and significant facts about world events and human evolution are indicated to the crowd through parables and imagery. Then it is said that when He was alone with his disciples He interpreted this imagery to them. In the Gospel of Mark we are on one occasion given a specific example of how the Christ spoke to the crowd in imagery and then interpreted it to His pupils.

> And He taught them many things in parables, and said to them in His teaching, "Listen! Behold, a sower went out to sow. And it happened as he sowed that one part fell by the path and the birds came and devoured it. And another part fell on stony ground, where there was not much soil, and it immediately shot up because it did not lie deep in the soil. And when the sun rose it was scorched and withered because it had no root.
>
> "And another part fell in thorns, and the thorns grew up and choked it, and it yielded no fruit.
>
> "And another part fell in the good ground and brought forth fruit, which sprang up and grew and yielded thirtyfold and sixtyfold and a hundredfold."
>
> And he said, "He who has ears to hear, let him hear."
>
> And when he was alone, his company together with the Twelve asked him about the parables. (Mark 4: 2–10.)

And to his more intimate pupils he spoke as follows,
"The sower sows the word.

"But in the case of those who heard the word that was
sown by the path, Satan comes immediately and takes away
the word that had been sown among them.

"Those who hear the word that was sown on stony
ground receive it immediately with joy. These have no root
in themselves but are children of the moment. Then when
they are afflicted or persecuted because of the word they immediately are confused and stumble.

"When by contrast it is sown among thorns some hear
it, but then worldly cares, the temptation of riches, and
other kinds of desires enter and choke the word, and it remains without fruit.

"Where it is sown on good ground there are people who
hear and receive the word, and it yields fruit, thirty, sixty
and a hundredfold." (Mark 4: 14-20.)

Here we have a perfect example of how Christ Jesus
taught. We are told how Buddha taught, and how Socrates
taught. Of the Buddha we can say in our Western language
that he carried earthly experience up into the heavenly
realm. It has often been said of Socrates that the tendency of
his teaching can best be characterized by saying that he
brought philosophy down from the heavens to earth in appealing directly to human earthly reason. In this way we can
picture clearly the relation of these two individualities to
their pupils.

Now how did Christ Jesus stand in relation to His pupils?
His relationship to the crowd was different from that toward
His own pupils. He taught the crowd in parable whereas for
His intimate pupils He interpreted the parables, telling
them what they were capable of understanding, of grasping
clearly through human reason. So if we want to characterize
the way Christ Jesus taught, we must speak of this in a more
complex manner. One characteristic feature is common to

73

all the Buddha's teaching; so the personal pupils of the Buddha are all of one kind. Similarly the entire world can become pupils of Socrates since Socrates wished only to elicit what lies hidden in the human soul. His disciples are therefore all of the same kind and Socrates has the same relationship to all. Christ Jesus, however, has two different kinds of relationships, one kind to His intimate pupils and another to the crowd. How may this be understood?

If we wish to understand the reason for this we must recognize clearly in our souls that the whole turning point of evolution had been reached at the time of the Mystery of Golgotha. The end of the period during which clairvoyance was the common possession of humanity was approaching. The further we go back in human evolution the more was the ancient clairvoyance that enabled men to see into the spiritual worlds the common possession of all mankind. How did they see into these worlds? Their vision took the form of perceiving the secrets of the cosmos in pictures, which were either conscious or unconscious imaginations. It was a dreamlike clairvoyance in the form of dreamlike imaginations, not in the rational concepts that people today make use of in the pursuit of knowledge. Both science and popular thinking which today make use of prosaic reasoning power and judgment were absent in those ancient times. In confronting the external world men did indeed see it, but they did not analyze it conceptually. They possessed no logic, nor did they make deductions in their thinking. Actually it is difficult for a man of today to imagine this because today one thinks about everything. But ancient man did not think in this way. He passed by objects and formed mental images of them; and in the intermediate state between sleeping and waking when he looked into his dreamlike imaginative world and saw pictures he was able to understand his mental images.

Let us envisage the matter more concretely. Picture to

yourselves how, many thousands of years ago, ancient man would have observed his environment. He would have been struck by the fact that a teacher was present who explained something to his pupils. A man of former times would have stood there and listened to the words the teacher was saying to his pupils. And if there had been several pupils present he would have heard how one receives the word with fervor, another takes it up but soon lets it fall, while a third is so absorbed in his own egoism that he does not listen. A man of former times would not have been able, for example, to have compared these three pupils in a rational manner. But when he was in the intermediate state between waking and sleeping, then the whole scene would have appeared again before his soul in the form of a picture. And he would have seen something, for example, like this: how a sower walks scattering seed; and this he would have really seen as a clairvoyant picture. He would have seen how one seed is thrown in good soil where it comes up well, a second seed he throws on poorer soil, and the third on stony soil. A smaller crop comes up from what was sown on the poor soil and nothing at all from the stony soil. Such a man of earlier times would not have said, as the man of today would, "One pupil takes up the words, another does not take them up at all," and so on. But in the intermediate state between sleeping and waking he saw the imaginative picture, and with it the explanation. He would never have spoken of it in any other way. If he had been asked to explain the relation of the teacher to his pupils he would have told about his clairvoyant vision. For him that was the reality, and also the explanation. And that is the way he would have talked.

Now the crowd facing Christ Jesus possessed indeed only the last remnant of ancient clairvoyance. But their souls were still well versed at listening to what was told to them in the form of pictures about the coming into being and the evolution of mankind. When Christ Jesus spoke to the

75

crowd He spoke as if He were speaking to people who still retained the last heritage of ancient clairvoyance and took it with them in their ordinary life of soul.

Who, then, were His intimate disciples? We have heard how the Twelve consisted of the seven sons of the Maccabean mother and the five sons of Mattathias. We have heard how throughout the whole history of the Hebrew people they had advanced to the point where they could vigorously assert their immortal ego. They were indeed the first whom Christ Jesus could choose Himself, appealing to that which lives in every human soul, living in it in such a way that it can become the new starting point for human development. To the crowd he spoke on the assumption that they would understand what they had preserved as a heritage from ancient clairvoyance. To His disciples He spoke on the assumption that they were the first who would be able to understand a little of what we today can say to human beings about higher worlds. It was thus a necessity for Christ Jesus during the whole of the turning point of time to speak in a different way when He was addressing the crowd from when He was speaking to His intimate pupils. The Twelve whom He drew to Himself He placed in the middle of the crowd. It was the task of Christ Jesus' closer circle of pupils to acquire that understanding, that rational understanding of things that belonged to the higher worlds and of the secrets of human evolution that in later times would become the common property of mankind. If we take what He said as a whole when He interpreted the parables for His pupils, we can say that He spoke also in a Socratic manner. For He drew forth what He said from the souls of each one of them, with the difference that Christ Jesus spoke of spiritual matters while Socrates spoke rather about the circumstances of earthly life and made use of ordinary logic. When Christ spoke to His intimate pupils about spiritual matters He did so in a Socratic manner. When the Buddha spoke to his disciples and expounded spiritual matters he showed how this was possible through illumination and through the sojourn of the human soul in the spiritual world. When Christ spoke to the crowd He spoke of the higher worlds in the way in which they formerly were experienced by ordinary human souls. He spoke to the crowd, as one might say, like a popular Buddha; to His intimate disciples He spoke like a higher Socrates, a spiritualized Socrates. Socrates drew forth from the souls of his pupils the individual earthly reason, whereas Christ drew forth heavenly reason from the souls of His disciples. The Buddha gave heavenly enlightenment to his pupils; Christ in His parables gave earthly enlightenment to the crowd.

I would ask you to give thought to these three pictures: Over there in the land of the Ganges there is the Buddha with his pupils—the antithesis of Socrates; over there in Greece is Socrates with his pupils—the antithesis of the Buddha. And then four or five centuries later there is this remarkable synthesis, this remarkable combination. Here you have before your souls one of the greatest examples of the regular, lawful development of human evolution. Human evolution proceeds step by step. Many of the things taught in years past in the early stages of spiritual science may have been thought by some people to be a kind of theory, a mere doctrine as, for example, when it was explained that the human soul should be thought of as the combined action of the sentient soul, intellectual soul and consciousness soul. Some people certainly make their judgments too quickly, indeed, a good deal more quickly even than those who take something that is merely a first draft and regard it as the finished product, a draft that was still awaiting further development. Such different judgments which we have actually experienced are all right as long as it is drawn to the attention of anthroposophists how they ought *not* to think. Sometimes we are confronted with blatant examples of how not to think, although many people believe we should indeed think like that. For example, this morning someone gave me a fine example of an odd kind of thinking which I am quoting here only as an example, though it is one that we should very much take to heart for the reason that we as anthroposophists should not only take notice of the world's shortcomings but should actually do something towards the consistent perfecting of the soul. So if I take what was told me this morning as an example, I do this not for a personal but for a spiritual reason that has wide application.

I was told that in a certain area of Europe a gentleman is living who at one time a long time ago had printed some pointless statements about the teachings that appear in Steiner's *Theosophy* as well as about his general relationship to the spiritual movement. Now it happened today that an acquaintance of this gentleman was criticized because his acquaintance, that is this particular gentleman, had published something like this. To which the acquaintance replied, "Why, my friend has just begun to study the writings of Dr. Steiner in an intensive manner." Yet this friend years before had passed judgment on these writings, and it is offered as an excuse that he is just beginning now to study them! This is a way of thinking that ought to be impossible within our movement. When some time in the future people write historically about our movement the question will certainly be asked, "Could it possibly be true that it occurred to someone to propose as an excuse that a man is only now beginning to acquaint himself with something on which he passed judgment years ago?" Such things are an integral part of anthroposophical education, and we shall make no progress unless it becomes generally accepted that such things must be unthinkable, absolutely unthinkable in our anthroposophical movement. For it is a necessary part of our inner honesty that we must be simply *unable* to think in this way. We can make no step forward in our search for truth if it is possible for us to pass such a judgment. And it is a duty for anthroposophists to take note of these things and not pass them by in an unloving manner while at the same time talking about the "universal love of mankind." In a higher sense it is indeed unloving toward a man if we forgive him something of this kind because we thereby condemn him to karmic meaninglessness and lack of existence after death. By drawing his attention to the impossible nature of such judgments we make easier his existence after death. This is the deeper meaning of the matter.

So we should not take it lightly when the truth is put forward in the first place in a simple manner, namely, that the human soul is composed of three members, the sentient soul, intellectual soul, and consciousness soul. Already in the course of the years it was emphasized how this fact has a much deeper significance than a mere dividing of the soul into three parts. It was pointed out how the various post-Atlantean cultures gradually developed: the ancient Indian, the primeval Persian and the Egypto-Babylonian-Chaldean cultures, the Greco-Latin culture and then ours. And it was shown how the essential characteristic of the Egyptian-Babylonian-Chaldean cultural epoch is the specific development of the true sentient soul of man. Similarly in the Greco-Latin era there was the specific culture of the intellectual soul, and in our era of the consciousness soul. So we are confronted with these three cultural epochs, which have their influence on the education and evolution of the human soul itself. These three soul members are not something that have been theoretically thought out, but are living realities developing progressively through successive epochs of time.

But everything must be linked. The earlier must always be carried over into the later, and in the same way the later must be foreshadowed in the earlier. In what cultural epoch do Socrates and the Buddha live? They live in the epoch of the intellectual soul; both have their task and their mission in that epoch.

The Buddha has the task of preserving the culture of the sentient soul from the previous, the third epoch, into the fourth. What the Buddha announces and his pupils take up into their hearts, is something destined to shine over from the third post-Atlantean period—the period of the sentient soul—into the era of the intellectual soul. In this way the era of the intellectual soul, the fourth post-Atlantean cultural period, could be warmed through by the glow and the light of the teachings of Buddha, by what was brought forth by the sentient soul, permeated as it was by clairvoyance. The Buddha was the great preserver of the sentient soul culture, bringing it forward right into the culture of the intellectual soul. What then was the mission of Socrates, who appeared somewhat later in time?

Socrates in the same way stands in the midst of the era of the intellectual soul. His appeal is made to the single human individuality, to something that can truly emerge only in our fifth cultural age. It was his task to foreshadow, though in a still abstract form, the era of the consciousness soul in the era of the intellectual soul. The Buddha preserves what came from the past, so that his message appears like a warming, shining light. Socrates anticipates what in his own time lies in the future, the characteristics of the consciousness soul era. So in his age it seemed to be somewhat prosaic, merely rational, even arid. Thus the third, fourth and fifth cultural epochs are telescoped in the fourth. The third is preserved by the Buddha, the fifth is anticipated by Socrates. West and East have the task of pointing up these two different missions—the East preserving the greatness of the past, while the West in an earlier era is anticipating what is to appear in a later one.

From the very ancient times in human evolution when the Buddha appeared time and again as the Boddhisattva, there is a straight path until the time when the Bodhisattva ascended to Buddhahood. There is a great and continuous development that comes to an end with the Buddha, and this really is an end because the Buddha undergoes his last incarnation on earth and never again descends to it. It was a great age that came to an end then, since it brought over from very ancient epochs what constituted the culture of the sentient soul of the third post-Atlantean cultural era and let it shine out again. If you will read the discourses of the Buddha from this point of view you will gain the right mood of soul and as a result the era of the intellectual soul will be valued by you in a different way. You will then return to the discourses of Buddha and say, "Everything here is of such a nature that it speaks directly to the human mind, but in the background is something that escapes from this mind and belongs to a higher world." This is the reason for that special rhythmic movement that ordinary rational men find objectionable which we find in the repetition of Buddha's discourses. This we can begin to understand only when we leave the physical for the etheric, entering in this way the first supersensible element behind the material. Anyone here who understands how much is active in the etheric body which stands behind the physical will also understand why so much in Buddha's discourses is repeated again and again. The repetitions must not be deleted from the discourses since such deletion takes away that special mood of soul that lives in them. Abstract-minded persons have done this in the belief that it is doing something helpful if they eliminate the repetitions and stick to the content. But it is important that they should be left just as the Buddha gave them.

If now we consider Socrates as he was, without all the wealth of material provided by the discoveries of natural science and the humanities since his day, and observe how he approaches the things of everyday life, we shall see how a man of the present time, when fortified by all the material of natural science, will find everywhere the Socratic method active in it. We expect it and need it. So we have a clear line beginning with Socrates and continuing into our own era, and this will grow ever more perfect in the future.

Thus there is one stream of human development that goes as far as the Buddha and ends with him; and there is another stream that begins with Socrates and goes on into the distant future. Socrates and the Buddha stand next to one another like the nuclei of two comets, if I may be allowed such an image. In the case of the Buddha, the light-filled comet's tail encircles the nucleus and points far back into the indeterminate perspectives of the past; in the case of Socrates the comet's tail of light encircles the nucleus in the same way but points far, far into the indeterminate distances of the future. Two diverging comets going in succession in opposite directions whose nuclei shine at the same time, this is the image I should like to use to illustrate how Socrates and the Buddha stand side by side.

Half a millennium passes, and something like a uniting of these two streams comes into being through Christ Jesus. We have already characterized this by putting a number of facts before our souls. Tomorrow we shall continue with this characterization so that we can answer the question, "How can we best characterize the mission of Christ Jesus in relation to the human soul?"

LECTURE 5

Yesterday we endeavored to place before our minds from a certain point of view the world-historical position that existed at the moment in time when the Mystery of Golgotha occurred. We tried to do this by presenting the picture of two significant leaders of mankind, the Buddha and Socrates, both of whom lived several centuries before the Mystery of Golgotha. In doing this we remarked that the Buddha represented something like the significant conclusion of one stream of evolution. There Buddha stands in the fifth or sixth century before the Mystery of Golgotha proclaiming what has since then been recognized as a deeply significant teaching. The revelation of Benares, that in a certain way encompasses and renews all that had been able to flow into human souls during thousands of years, was proclaimed in the only way it could be half a millennium before the Mystery of Golgotha. We can see even more clearly how far the Buddha represented the great conclusion of one cosmic stream when we place before our minds his great predecessor who recedes far back into the twilight of human evolution: Krishna, who in quite a different sense appears to us as the final moment of a revelation thousands of years old. Krishna can be placed several centuries before the Buddha, but that is not the issue here. The main point is that the more we allow the being of Krishna and the being of the Buddha to affect us, the more clearly do we recognize that in Krishna what was later to be proclaimed by the Buddha appears in an even brighter light, whereas with Buddha, as we wish to demonstrate in a moment, in a certain way it comes to an end.

The name "Krishna" embraces something that for

many thousands of years has shone into the spiritual development of mankind. If we immerse ourselves in all that is meant by the proclamation of Krishna, we look up into the sublime heights of human spiritual evolution, instilling the feeling within us that nothing can possibly surpass, nothing can enhance what is contained in, what resounds from Krishna's revelation. What resounds from this revelation of Krishna is a kind of climax; in saying this we are attributing to the person of Krishna what also was revealed by others before him. For it is indeed true that everything that had been given out gradually for thousands of years before his time by those who were given the task of becoming the bearers of knowledge was renewed, summed up and brought to a conclusion in the revelations of Krishna to his people. If we take into consideration how Krishna speaks about the divine spiritual worlds and the relation of these worlds to mankind, and about the course of cosmic events, and if we also consider the spirituality to which we ourselves must rise if we wish to penetrate the deeper meaning of the teaching of Krishna, then we may say that only one event in the whole subsequent development of humanity can in even a slight degree be compared with it. We may say of the revelation of Krishna that it is in a certain sense an occult teaching. Why occult? It is occult for the simple reason that few people can achieve the inner capacity to ascend to those spiritual heights where understanding can be gained. There is no need to keep secret what Krishna revealed in an external way, to lock it up in a safe, so that it stays "occult"; it remains occult for no other reason than that too few people rise to the heights to which they must rise if they are to understand it. However widely such revelations as those of Krishna are disseminated among the people and put into their hands, they still remain occult. For they can be brought out of the realm of the occult not by disseminating them among the people, but only when there are souls who

84

can rise high enough to be able to unite with them. It is true that such revelations hover above us at a certain spiritual height, yet they speak to us as if from a high point of spirituality. Anyone who simply picks up the words that are contained in such revelations should by no means believe he understands them, not even if he is a learned man of the twentieth century. It is entirely comprehensible that it is widely asserted today that there is no occult teaching. This is understandable because those who say such things do indeed possess the words, and with them think they have everything. But it is in the very nature of occult teaching that they do not understand what they possess.

Earlier I said that there is just one thing that can be compared with the teaching of Krishna, and indeed what we associate with the name "Krishna" can be compared with what may remind us of three later names which are in a certain sense closely connected with us—though in the case of these three the method, conceptual and philosophical, is quite different. I am referring to everything that in recent years has been linked to the names of Fichte, Schelling and Hegel, and the teachings of these men have a slight resemblance to other "occult teachings" of mankind. For though we can undoubtedly acquire the writings of Fichte, Schelling, and Hegel, it cannot be denied that in the widest sense of the words they have remained occult teaching. Truly they have remained occult to this day. There are very few people who wish to achieve any kind of relation to what these three men have written. From a certain kind of what I may call philosophical courtesy, there is today in certain circles some talk about Hegel again; and if something is said like what I have just said myself, then the reply is made that after all there really are some people who busy themselves with Hegel. However, if one listens to what these people say and what they contribute to the understanding of Hegel, then we are all the more compelled to the view that for these people Hegel has remained an occult teaching. What shines out towards us from the East from Krishna appears again in Fichte, Schelling and Hegel in an abstract conceptual way, and it is not easy to notice the similarity; indeed, it requires a special constitution of soul to be able to do so. I should like to speak candidly about this and state clearly what is required.

When a man of today who believes he has enjoyed not an average but a superior education takes up a philosophical work by Fichte or Hegel he believes he is reading something concerned only with the development of advanced concepts. Most people will agree that it is difficult really to warm up to it, if, for example, they turn to Hegel's *Encyclopaedia of the Philosophical Sciences* and read for the first time about being, nonbeing, becoming, existence, and the like. We have probably heard it said that in this work a man has cooked up a collection of highly abstract concepts, beautiful enough, no doubt, but providing nothing capable of kindling warmth in heart or soul. I have known many people who after three or four pages of this particular work have promptly closed the book. But they are not at all prepared to admit that perhaps the guilt lies in themselves that they do not warm up and have avoided the struggles that have to be endured in going from hell to heaven. This they do not willingly admit. Yet it is possible by means of these so-called "abstract concepts" to experience a veritable life-struggle, and to feel not only a living warmth but the whole range of feeling from the most extreme cold to the highest soul-warmth. Then one can come to feel that these things are written not in simply abstract concepts but in the heart's blood.

We may compare what radiates over to us from Krishna with what is regarded as the newest evolutionary phase of the human ascent toward the spiritual heights. Yet there is a significant difference. What we meet with in Fichte, Schelling and Hegel, these most mature thinkers of Christianity, we meet with in a pre-Christian era, in the form it had to take then, in Krishna. For what is Krishna's revelation? It is something that can never again be repeated, whose greatness of its kind and in its own way can never be surpassed. If we have an understanding for such things we may have a conception, an idea of the strength of that spiritual light that shines over to us, if we let such things affect us as are connected with the culture from which Krishna emerged. If we do this, if we allow words like the following to influence us (to take a few examples from the *Bhagavad Gita*) where Krishna indicates in words his real being, we arrive at thoughts, feelings and emotions that will be characterized later. Thus in the tenth canto Krishna speaks as follows:

> I am the spirit of creation, its beginning, its center and its end. Among all beings I am always the noblest of all that has come into being; among spiritual beings I am Vishnu, I am the sun among the stars; among the lights I am the moon; among the elements I am fire; among the mountains I am the lofty Meru; among the water I am the great cosmic sea, among the rivers I am the Ganges, among the multitude of trees I am Ashvattha; in the true sense of the word I am the ruler of men and of all the beings that live; among the serpents I am the one that is eternal, the very ground of existence itself!

Let us take another example from the same culture, which we find in the Vedas. The Devas were gathered around the throne of the Almighty, and in deep reverence they ask who he himself is. Then the Almighty, that is to say the cosmic god in the old Indian sense, answered:

> If there were another than I, I would describe myself through him. I have been from all eternity and through all eternity I shall be. I am the primal cause of everything, of all that is in West, in East, in North and South; I am the cause

of all that is in the heights above and in the depths below. I am all, I am more ancient than anything that is. I am the ruler of rulers, I am the truth itself. I am revelation itself, and the cause of revelation. I am knowledge, I am piety, I am the law. I am almighty!

And when, as the ancient document records, it was asked what was the cause of all things, the answer was given:

> The cause of the world, it is fire; it is the sun and it is also the moon. It is also this pure Brahman and this water and this highest of all creatures. All moments and all weeks and all months and all centuries and all millennia and all millions of years have proceeded from him, have emerged from his radiant personality which no one can comprehend, neither above nor below nor in the circumference, nor in the center, here where we stand!

Such words sound over to us from very ancient times, and we surrender ourselves to them. If we approach these words without preconceptions, how do we feel in relation to them? Certain things are said in the words; we have seen that Krishna says something about himself. And things are said about the cosmic God and about cosmic origins. From the tone of these thoughts, as they sound forth through these words, things are said that could never have been expressed in a greater or more significant way. And one knows that they never could have been spoken in a greater or more significant manner. That is to say, something was placed into human evolution that must stand just as it is and be accepted as it is since it has come to a conclusion. And wherever people in later times have thought about such things, and may perhaps have believed in accordance with methods employed in these later times that one thing or another could have been expressed in clearer concepts or could have been modified in one way or another, they have nevertheless been unable to say it better. They have never done so. Indeed if anyone wished to say something better about precisely these things, it would be sheer presumption.

Let us first consider the passage of the Bhagavad Gita where Krishna, so to speak, characterizes his own nature. What is he really characterizing? His way of speaking is truly remarkable. He says of his nature that he is the spirit of all that has come into being, that he is among the heavenly spirits Vishnu, among the stars the sun, among the lights the moon, among the elements the fire, and so on. If we wish to paraphrase this and compress it into a formula we can say that Krishna points to himself as the essence, the entity of all things. He *is* this entity in such a way that it represents always the purest, the most divine kind of nature. Hence, according to this passage, if we penetrate beyond the actual things and seek to find behind them the nature of their true being, we arrive at the being of Krishna. If we take a number of plants of the same species and look for the entity of this species, which is not in itself visible but comes to expression in the single plant forms, and ask what lies behind them as their essence, the answer is: Krishna! But we must not think of this being as identical with any single plant but must think of him as the highest and purest element in the form. Thus we have not only what the essence is, but this essence in its highest, noblest, purest form.

So of what is Krishna actually speaking? Of nothing else but what a man can recognize as his own essence when he sinks into himself; not his being as it appears to him in ordinary life, but something that lies *behind* man and the human soul as they manifest themselves in life. He speaks of the human essence that is within us because the true human essence is at one with the universe. This is by no means a knowledge that works egotistically within Krishna. It is something in Krishna that wishes to point to the highest in man, something that may perceive itself as identical and at one with what lives as being in all things.

Just as we speak today for our own age, so Krishna spoke to his own age of what he had in mind for his culture. If today we look into our own being we first of all glimpse the ego as you will find it pictured in the book *Knowledge of the Higher Worlds and its Attainment*. We distinguish the ordinary ego from the higher, supersensible ego which does not appear in the world of sense. This supersensible ego appears in such a manner that it is not only in us but is at the same time poured out over the being of all things. So when we speak of our higher ego, the higher being dwelling in man, we do not speak of what a man says when he says in his customary manner "I am," although in our language it has the same sound. In Krishna's mouth it would not have had the same sound. He is speaking of the nature of the human soul as it would have been interpreted in that day, in the same way as we today speak of the ego.

How did it come about that Krishna expresses something that is so similar to what we express when we speak of the highest of which we have knowledge? This was possible because the culture out of which Krishna emerged was preceded for thousands of years by a clairvoyant culture, because human beings were accustomed to rising to clairvoyant vision when they looked into the being of things. And we can understand a language such as resounds here to us from the *Bhagavad Gita* when we look upon it as the close of the old clairvoyant view of the world, when we recognize that when a man in those ancient times passed into the intermediate state between sleeping and waking that was at that time common to all human beings he was not placed among things in such a way that they were "here" and he was outside them, as is the case in ordinary sense perception. He felt himself poured out over all things, felt himself in all beings and at one with them. It was with the best of things that he felt himself to be at one, and his best was in all things. And if you do not start out from an abstract feeling and an abstract perception in the way customary with men of the present time but rather start out from the old way of feeling and perception as we have just characterized them, then you will understand such words as resound over to us from Krishna in the *Bhagavad Gita.* If then you ask how men with the old clairvoyance perceived themselves, you will understand them and realize that in the same way that a man, when his etheric body is freed through spiritual scientific training, feels himself spread and poured out into what lives in everything, so did the man of former times experience this as a natural condition, although not in the same way as would now be the case as a result of spiritual scientific training. Ancient men felt themselves to be inside things, and this condition came about by itself without their volition. And when these revelations were shaped into forms and what had been seen was expressed in beautiful, wonderful words, then something appeared like, for example, these revelations of Krishna. For this reason it could also be said that Krishna spoke to his fellowmen in this way, "I wish to proclaim in words what the best of us have perceived when they were in the supersensible worlds and how the best of us have perceived their relationship to the world. In future times such men as these will no longer be found, and you yourselves cannot be as your ancestors were. I wish to put into words what these ancestors perceived, so that it will endure, because humanity can no longer possess this as a natural condition."

Thus something which had belonged to mankind for thousands of years was brought in words such as were possible at that time in the form of the revelations of Krishna so that mankind in subsequent ages might possess this revelation of what they were no longer able to perceive for themselves.

Other sayings can also be interpreted in a similar manner. Let us suppose that at a period when Krishna was giving his revelations a pupil had stood before his initiate teacher and asked him, "What lies behind the things which my eyes see, can you, my initiated teacher tell me?" The initiated teacher might well have answered, "Behind those things which are now seen by your external, material eyes, lies the spiritual, the supersensible. But in former times men could still see the supersensible while they were in their normal condition. They were able to look into the nearest supersensible world, the etheric world that borders on our material world. Here in this world is to be found the cause of everything that is material, and these men of old were able to see what this cause is. In our time I can do no more than express in words what could in earlier times be seen, 'It is fire, it is the sun!' But not the sun as it now appears, for what can now be seen by the eye was precisely what for ancient clairvoyants could least of all be seen. The white fiery globe of the sun was darkness for them, while the effects of the sun were spread over all space. The radiations of the sun's aura in many-colored light pictures flowed in and out of each other, coming forth from each other, in such a way that when they merged into things they became immediately creative light. It is the sun, it is also the moon (though this too was seen in a different manner), for pure Brahman is altogether in it."

What is pure Brahman? When we breathe in the air and breathe it out again the materialistic person believes he is only inhaling oxygen. But that is a delusion; with every breath we inhale and exhale spirit. The spirit that lives in the air we breathe penetrates into us and goes out from us again. And when an old clairvoyant saw that, he did not, like the materialist, believe that he was breathing in oxygen. That is a materialistic prejudice. The clairvoyant of ancient times was aware that the etheric element of the spirit, Brahman, from whom all life comes, was being inhaled. In the same way that today we believe that life comes from the oxygen in the air, so did ancient man know that life comes

92

from Brahman; and in that he takes up Brahman, he lives. The purest Brahman is the source of our life.

And of what nature are the conceptual heights to which this very ancient, this ether-like, light-like wisdom aspires? Today people believe they are able to think with great subtlety. But when we see how people jumble up everything in a higgledy-piggledy way as soon as they try to explain something, then we lose all respect for the thinking of today, especially for its *logical* thinking. At this point I really must engage in a short discussion that may seem abstract. I shall make it as short as possible.

Let us suppose that we encounter an animal that has a mane and is yellow; then we call this animal a lion. Now we begin to ask, "What is a lion?" The answer, "A beast of prey." Next we ask, "What is a beast of prey?" Answer, "A mammal." We ask further, "What is a mammal?" Answer, "A living creature." And so we continue describing one thing through another. Most people believe they are being very lucid when they go on asking ever more questions in the same way as they asked about the lion, the mammal and so on. And people often ask similar questions about spiritual matters, even about the highest spiritual things, in just the same way as they ask what a lion is, what a beast of prey is, and the rest. And at the end of lectures, when slips of paper are handed in with questions, questions such as these are asked countless numbers of times, for example, "What is God?" "How did the world begin?" "How will the world end?" There are many people who have no wish to know anything at all beyond these questions. They ask them in just the same way as they ask, "What is a lion?" and so on.

People think that what is valid for everyday life must also be equally valid for the highest things. They do not take into consideration that it is just the highest things that are of such a nature that we cannot ask such questions about them. If we proceed from one thing to another, from the lion to the beast of prey and so on, we must eventually come to something that cannot be described in this way, when there is no longer any sense in asking, what is this? For in this kind of questioning a predicate is sought for the subject. But when we reach the highest being, this being can be comprehended only through itself. From a logical point of view it is absolutely meaningless to ask the question, "What is God?" Everything can be led upward to the highest, but to the highest *no* predicate can be added, for the answer would have to be: God is . . ., and God would then have to be described in terms of something higher. So the question itself would involve the strangest contradiction possible.

The fact that this question is still invariably asked today shows how highly exalted Krishna was when he appeared in a very early epoch and spoke as follows, "The Devas gather around the throne of the Almighty, and in deep devotion ask who He Himself is. Then He answers, 'If there were anyone else other than I myself, I should describe myself through him.'" But this He does not do; He does not describe Himself through another. So we also, as we could say, like the Devas, are led in devotion and humility to this ancient and holy culture, and admire its grandiose logical elevation which it did not achieve through thinking but through the old clairvoyance. In those times people knew at once that when they reached the causes then questioning must cease. The causes must be *perceived*. At this point we stand in admiration in front of what has come down to us from those very ancient times, as though the spirits who transmitted it to us wished to say to us, "The times have gone when men could see directly into the spiritual worlds, nor will they be able to do so in the future. But we wish to record what we can aspire to, something that at one time was granted to human clairvoyance."

So we find recorded in the *Bhagavad Gita* and in the

94

Vedas all those things that were brought together by Krishna as in a kind of conclusion. Such things cannot be surpassed, though they will be perceived again when clairvoyance is renewed. But they will never be perceived through those faculties that have been attained by men in subsequent times. For this reason it is always correct to say that if we remain within the realm of contemporary culture, an external culture whose content is determined by sense perception, we shall never again attain to that ancient sacred revelation which found its conclusion in Krishna unless it is attained through a trained clairvoyance. But through its own evolution through spiritual science the soul can again raise itself and attain it again. What was at one time given to man in a normal way, if I can express myself in this way, is not now given to mankind in ordinary life and cannot be attained by him under natural conditions. It is for this reason that these truths came down to us. When there are thinkers like Fichte, Schelling and Hegel who reached the highest possible purity in their thinking, then we can meet with these things again, not indeed as life-filled as they were nor with the direct personal impact of Krishna, but in the form of ideas—though never in the way in which they were understood in the time of the old clairvoyance. And, as I have often stated, it was a spiritual necessity that the old clairvoyance should slowly and gradually die out in the post-Atlantean era.

If we look back to the ancient Indian civilization, the first post-Atlantean cultural period, we may say that no records are extant from this epoch, for at that time men still could see into the spiritual world. Only through the Akasha Chronicle can there be rediscovered what was then revealed to mankind. It was a lofty revelation. But then mankind sank down lower and lower. In the old Persian epoch, the second post-Atlantean cultural period, though the revelations still continued they had lost their original purity. They were still less pure in the third cultural period, that of ancient Egypt. If we wish to visualize what were the real conditions of the time we must bear in mind that as far as the first cultural epochs are concerned no records exist, and this is true for all the peoples of that age, whether or not a cultural epoch has been called after them. If we speak of the ancient Indian culture we are referring to a culture from which nothing has come down to us in writing. It is just the same with the primeval Persian culture. Written records exist only from the Egyptian-Babylonian-Chaldean culture, which belongs to the third cultural period. But during the period of the unfolding of the primeval Persian culture within Indian culture there was a second Indian period, running parallel to the old Persian. And yet a third period began in India contemporary with the Egyptian-Babylonian-Chaldean culture, and it was during this period that the first written records began to be kept. These first records date from the latter part of this third culture. Such records are, for example, those contained in the Vedas, which then penetrated into external life. It is these records which also speak of Krishna.

So no one should believe when he speaks of written records that they go back to the first Indian cultural epoch. Everything contained in the documents are records first written down in the third period of ancient India, for the reason that precisely in the third period the old clairvoyance was dying out more and more. These are the records assembled around the person of Krishna. Thus ancient India tells us something that can be externally investigated. If we examine things fundamentally, everything agrees with what can be discovered in the external documents. As the third world age came to an end and men lost what they had originally possessed, Krishna appeared on the scene to preserve what otherwise would have been lost.

When tradition says that Krishna appeared in the third

world-age, what age is meant by this? This age is what we call the Egypto-Chaldean cultural epoch. The Indian-Oriental teaching of Krishna accords perfectly with what we have been characterizing. When the old clairvoyance and all its treasures were on the point of being lost, then Krishna appeared and revealed them so that they could be preserved into later times. Thus Krishna is the conclusion of something great and powerful. And everything that has been said here over the years agrees entirely with what is given also in the oriental documents if we read them rightly. It is pure nonsense to talk in this context of "occidental" and "oriental," because this is only a matter of language, of vocabulary. What is important is that we speak with a full understanding of that which we proclaim. And the more you go into what has been given out over the years, the more you will see that it is in complete agreement with all the documents of the Orient.

So Krishna stands there as a conclusion. Then, a few centuries later, comes the Buddha. In what sense is the Buddha, if we may so express it, the other pole of this conclusion? In what relation does the Buddha stand to Krishna?

Let us place before our souls what we have just spoken of as characteristic of Krishna: great powerful clairvoyant revelations of primordial ages, couched in such words that men of future times will be able to understand and feel and sense in them the ancient clairvoyance of humanity. Krishna's revelation, as he stands before us, is something that men can accept and can say to each other that herein is contained the wisdom of the spiritual world that lies behind the sense world, the world of causes and spiritual facts. This wisdom is expressed in great powerful words in Krishna's revelations. If we immerse ourselves in the Vedas, in all that we can sum up in conclusion as the revelation of Krishna, then we may say that this is the world in which man is at home, the world which lies behind what our eyes can see, our ears hear, our hands grasp, and so on. Yes, the human soul belongs to the world revealed by Krishna.

How could the human soul itself feel in the course of subsequent centuries? It could perceive how these marvelous revelations of an older time spoke about the true, spiritual, celestial home of mankind. It could then look into all that surrounded it. It saw with eyes, heard with ears, grasped things with the sense of touch; it could think with the intellect about things, the intellect that never penetrates into the spiritual element proclaimed in the revelation of Krishna. And the soul could say to itself, "There is an ancient holy teaching from times past which tells of a world, our spiritual home which lies all around us, around that world which is all that we now recognize. We no longer live in that spiritual home, we have been expelled from that world of which Krishna spoke so magnificently."

Then comes the Buddha. How does he speak of the marvels of the world spoken of by Krishna to human souls which could perceive only what eyes can see and ears hear? He says, "Certainly you live in the world of the senses. The yearning that drives you from incarnation to incarnation has led you into this world. But I am telling you of that path which can lead you out of this world and into that world of which Krishna spoke. I am telling you about the path through which you will be redeemed from the world that is not the world of Krishna." Buddha's teaching in these later centuries resounds like a kind of nostalgia for the world of Krishna. In this respect the Buddha seems to us like the last successor of Krishna, as Krishna's successor who had to come. And if the Buddha himself had spoken of Krishna, how would he have been able to speak about him? He would have said something like this, "I have come to proclaim to you again the greater one who was my predecessor. Turn your mind backward to the Krishna who was greater than I, and you will see what you can attain if you leave this world which is not your true spiritual home. I will show you the path by which you can redeem yourselves from the world of sense. I lead you back to Krishna.''

The Buddha could have spoken in this way, but he did not use these exact words. Nevertheless he did say them in a somewhat different form when he said, "In the world in which you live there is suffering, there is suffering, there is suffering. Birth is suffering. Age is suffering. Illness is suffering. Death is suffering. To be apart from that which one loves is suffering. To be bound to that which one does not love is suffering. The longing for that which one loves but may not attain is suffering." And so he gave his Eightfold Path. It was a teaching that did not go beyond that of Krishna because in fact it was the same teaching as the one given by Krishna. "I have come after him who is greater than I, and I will show you the way back to him who is greater than I." These are the world-historical tones that ring forth to us from the land of the Ganges.

Now let us go a little further toward the West, and place once more before our souls the figure of the Baptist, and remember the words that the Buddha could have spoken, "I have come after Krishna who is greater than I; and I will show you the way back to him, away from the world bereft of the divine of which Krishna spoke. Turn your minds backward!"

Now consider the figure of the Baptist. How did he speak, how did he express his views? How did he express the facts he had received from the spiritual world? He too pointed to another, but he did not say, as the Buddha could have said, "I have come after him." On the contrary he said, "*After* me there will come one greater than I." (Mark 1: 7.) This is what the Baptist said. Nor did he say, "Here in the world is suffering, and I wish to lead you to something that is not of this world." No, he said, "Change your way of thinking. Do not continue to look backward, but look forward. When He comes who is greater than I the time will be fulfilled. Then the divine world will enter into the world of suffering. And what was lost of the revelations of past times will enter in a new way into human souls." (Matt. 5: 2.)

So the successor of Krishna is the Buddha, and John the Baptist is the forerunner of Christ Jesus. Thus everything is reversed. We are faced with the six hundred years that elapsed between these two events, and we have before us the two comets, with their nuclei: the one comet pointing backward with Krishna as nucleus together with the one who leads men backward, the Buddha. Then we have the other comet pointing forward, with Christ as its nucleus together with him who stands before us as the forerunner. If, in the best sense, you recognize the Buddha as the successor of Krishna, and John the Baptist as the forerunner of Christ Jesus, then this formula expresses in the simplest way what took place in human evolution around the time of the Mystery of Golgotha. It is in this way that we should look at things, and then we can understand them.

All this has no bearing on any religious confession, nor should it be linked with any particular religion. These are facts of world history. No one who understands them in their innermost depths can present them or will ever present them in a different way. Do such statements impair in any way any revelation ever given to mankind? It is curious that it is sometimes said that we assign in some way a higher place to Christianity than to other religions. Do such words as "higher" or "deeper" have any meaning in this context? Are not such words as "higher" or "lower," "larger," or "smaller" the most abstract words we can use? Are we praising Krishna any less than do those who put him higher than Christ? We refrain from using such words as "higher" or "less high," and wish only to characterize these matters in accordance with the truth. It is not a matter of whether we place Christianity higher or lower, but whether we characterize in the right way what belongs to Krishna. Look up all that has been said about Krishna, and ask yourselves whether anyone else has ever said anything about Krishna "higher" than what has been presented here. Everything else is idle talk. But truth comes to light when there begins to be active that feeling for truth that goes to the essence of things.

Here when we are characterizing the simplest and grandest of the Gospels we have the opportunity of studying the whole position of the Christ as a cosmic and earthly being. It was therefore necessary to go into the greatness of what came to its conclusion centuries before the Mystery of Golgotha, in which the new morning-glow of the future of humanity dawned.

LECTURE 6

Yesterday an attempt was made to give you an idea of Krishna's revelation and its relation to what entered later into human evolution, the revelation through the Christ. It was especially noted how the revelation of Krishna can appear to us as the conclusion of the clairvoyant, the primitive clairvoyant epoch of human development. If we once more place before our souls from this point of view the understanding we obtained yesterday about the revelation of Krishna as a conclusion, we may say that whatever was gained through this revelation is still present in human evolution, but in a certain way it has reached an end and can go no further. Some teachings handed down at that time must be accepted during all subsequent evolution just as they were given then.

Now it is necessary for us to study the peculiar nature of this revelation from one particular point of view. We might say that it does not really reckon with time and the sequence of time. Everything that does not reckon with time as a real factor is already contained in Krishna's teaching. What do we mean by this?

Every spring we see the plants spring forth from the earth, we see them grow and ripen, bring forth fruit and drop their seeds, and from these seeds when they have been laid in the ground we see similar plants begin to grow again in the same way, come to maturity and again develop their seeds. This process is repeated year after year. If we reckon with the time span that man is able to survey we must say that we are here concerned with a real repetition. The lilies of the valley, the primroses and hyacinths look the same

102

every year. Their nature is repeated within them every year in the same way, in the same form. We can ascend further to the animal kingdom in a certain way, and we shall still find something similar in it. When we consider the individual animal, the separate species of lions, hyenas, the separate species of monkeys, we find that every creature is from the beginning directed to become what it does become. So we may with a certain justification say that no education is possible among the animals. Although some foolish persons have recently begun to apply all kinds of educational and pedagogical concepts to animals, this cannot be considered as something essential, nor does it lead to a correct characterization of animals. When we have short time-spans in mind we see this repetition in nature fundamentally confirmed, in the same way as we see how spring, summer, autumn and winter repeat themselves regularly through the centuries. Only when we consider really large spans of time, so large that they cannot in the first place be observed by man, would we see something resembling the need to take account of the concept of time. Then we should see how in the far distant past things happened differently from the way they do now, and we should, for example, be able to take into account the fact that the present way in which the sun rises and sets will in the far distant future be different. But these are realms which will come into our view only when we enter into the field of true spiritual science. But as regards what man is first of all able to observe, for example the field of astronomy, the fact of recurrence, the recurrence of the same or similar, holds good, as we can especially notice in the annual recurrence of plant forms. With this kind of recurrence time has no special significance; time itself, as time, is essentially not a real, active factor.

It is different when we think of individual human lives. As you all know, we also divide human life into successive, recurring periods. We distinguish one such period from birth to the coming of the second teeth, or about the seventh year, then a period from the seventh to the fourteenth year, to puberty, then one from the fourteenth to the twenty-first year, and so on. In short, we distinguish successive seven-year periods in individual human lives; and it is quite true to say that in these seven-year periods certain things recur. But far more striking than the mere recurrence is something else, the constant changing, the progress that is actually made. For human nature is quite different in the second period of seven years from what it was in the first period; and again in the third period it is different. We cannot say that in the case of man the first seven-year period repeats itself in the second, as we can say that the plant repeats itself in another plant. We can see that time as it passes plays a real role in human life. It has a meaning.

When we thus come to see how what is significant for the individual human being is applicable to all mankind, we can say that in the consecutive periods of evolution this can in a sense be seen to be true for both the individual and for humanity as a whole. We need not go beyond the post-Atlantean epoch. Here we differentiate in this era the ancient Indian or first post-Atlantean cultural epoch, the Old Persian as the second, the Egypto-Chaldean as the third, the Greco-Roman as the fourth and our own as the fifth. Two more epochs will follow ours, until there is again a great catastrophe. This evolutionary progress in successive epochs does often show similarities that can be compared in a certain way with the kind of recurrence that may be observed, for example, in the plant kingdom. We see how these periods run their course so that in a certain respect at the beginning of each epoch humanity receives certain revelations; a stream of spiritual life is given to mankind as an impulse, in the same way as the plants of the earth receive an impulse in springtime. Then we see how a further development is built on the first impulse, how it bears fruit and then dies away when the period comes to an end, as plants wither at the approach of winter. However, in addition, something appears during the successive epochs that is similar to the progress of an individual human being, and of this we can say that time plays a significant role, and it proves to be a real factor. It is not only the case that in the second, the Old Persian epoch, seeds are again planted, as was the case in the first epoch, or that in the third epoch the same thing happened as in the first. The impulses are always different, always at a higher level and always new, in just the same way that in human life the seven-year periods can be differentiated, and there is progress.

Now that which came to humanity in the course of time came in such a way that we could say that the things which comprise the sum total of human knowledge were opened up to man slowly and gradually. Not all the streams of peoples and nations always had the same perceptions of things at the same time. Thus we see that in that human evolutionary stream that came to an end at about the time of the Mystery of Golgotha, the sense for time as a real factor was missing. Indeed, in all Eastern knowledge this sense of time as a real factor was fundamentally missing. Characteristically the Eastern knowledge has a sense for the recurrence of the same. Therefore everything that is concerned with recurrence is magnificently grasped by the knowledge of the East.

When we think of this recurrence of the same in successive cultural epochs, what is it that comes into consideration? Take, for example, the question of plant growth. We see how in springtime the plants shoot forth from the earth; we witness their "creation." We see how these plants grow and flourish until they reach a kind of culmination. Then they wither, and in withering they carry in themselves the seed for a new plant. Thus we have to do here with a threefold process: coming into being, growth and flourishing, and then withering, and this withering is accompanied by the production of the seed of a similar plant. When time does not come into question, when it is a question of recurrence, then this principle of recurrence is best understood as a triad. It was the special talent of Oriental wisdom, pre-Christian wisdom, to understand recurring development as a triad. The grandeur of this ancient world view was limited by what we may think of as a predisposition in favor of events that recur and are timeless. And when this world view comes to a conclusion, trinities confront us everywhere, and fundamentally these represent the clairvoyant perception of what lies behind coming into being, passing away, and renewal. Brahma, Shiva, and Vishnu, this trinity of creative forces is the foundation of all things. In the time preceding Krishna's revelation it was recognized as a trinity that could be perceived through clairvoyance, and it was seen as Brahma, Vishnu and Shiva. The image of this trinity exists wherever time is seen only as the successive recurrence of the same.

The significance of a new era is recognized when the gift of seeing events in historical perspective arises, that is, when time is taken into account in relation to evolution, when time is looked upon as a real factor. It was a special task of Western knowledge to develop a historical sense, to penetrate into the truths of history. And the two streams in human evolution coming from East and West differ in that the East looks at the world unhistorically, while the West, prompted by a new impulse, begins to look at the world from a historical point of view. It was the world view of the Hebrews that gave the first impulse to this historical viewpoint.

Let us now consider together what the essential elements of the Oriental world view actually are. We are always told of recurring world ages, of what happens at the beginning of the first and at the end of the first cosmic age. Then we are told of the beginning of the second world age, and its end, then the beginning of the third and its end. And the secret of world development is correctly presented when it is said that when the ancient culture of the third world age had become dry and arid and the culture had entered the phase of autumn and winter, then there appeared Krishna. The son of Vasudeva and Devaki, his task was to sum up for later ages, namely for the fourth period, what could be carried from the third into the fourth period as the germ, the new seed for that period. The individual world ages appear to us like successive years in the life of a plant. In the Oriental world view the cycles of time, which constantly recur, are the essential element.

Now let us compare these world views in their timelessness, their profoundest aspect, with what confronts us in the Old Testament. What a mighty difference we find from the world views of the East! Here we perceive as an essential part of this view a real continuous line in time. We are first led to Genesis, to the Creation, and linked to Creation is the whole history of mankind. We see a continuous sequence through the seven days of Creation, through the era of the patriarchs, from Abraham down through Isaac and Jacob, everything developing, everything a part of history. Where is there any recapitulation? The first day of Creation is by no means repeated in an abstract way in the second. The patriarchs are not repeated in the prophets, nor does the era of the kings repeat the era of the judges. In due course comes the time of the captivity. We are everywhere led through an entire dramatic process, in which time plays a real part as it does in an individual human life. Irrespective of what is repeated time is shown as a real factor in all that happens. The special element in the picture presented by the Old Testament is progress. The Old Testament is the first great example of a historical approach to events, and it is this historical approach that was bequeathed to the West.

Men learn only slowly and gradually what in the course

of time has been revealed to them; and we may say that in a certain sense when there are new revelations there is a kind of reversion to what had gone before. Great and significant things were revealed at the beginning of the theosophical movement. But it was an extraordinary feature of this revelation that the historical approach permeated the movement very little. You can convince yourselves of this especially if you glance at Sinnett's *Esoteric Buddhism*, which in other respects is an excellent and meritorious book. All the chapters in it that are pervaded by history will be found acceptable by the Western mind. But side by side with this is another element that we may call an "unhistorical" element, curious passages in which large and small cycles are spoken of, the procession of rounds and races, where the material is presented in such a way that recurrence is of central importance—how the third round follows after the second, how one root-race follows after the other root-race, one subrace follows after the other subrace, and so on. One really becomes caught up in a kind of working of a clock, and the greatest importance is given to recurrence. This was a reversion to a kind of thinking that had already been outgrown by mankind, for the way of thinking suited to western culture is in truth historical.

What is the consequence of this historical element that belongs to Western culture? Precisely the knowledge of the one focus of all earthly development. The Orient regarded development as similar to the process of plant growth that recurs every year. Thus the individual great initiates appeared in each period and repeated—at all events it was what they repeated that was especially stressed—what had been done earlier. It was particularly emphasized in an abstract manner how each initiate was only a particular form of the one who continues his development from epoch to epoch. There was in the East a special interest in picturing how this continuous development of the same also is easily seen in the plant world as the form reveals itself each year, and the individual years are not distinguished from each other. Only in one particular case do people notice that there is a difference from year to year. If someone wants to describe a lily or a vine leaf it is of no consequence whether the plant grew in 1857 or 1867, for lilies all resemble each other if they belong to a particular variety of lily. But when what we may think of as the general, recurring, identical "Apollonian" element passes over into the "Dionysian," even in the realm of plant life, then we attach special importance to the fact that individual "vintages" do differ, and it becomes important to distinguish the different years. In all other cases no one cares whether a lily flowered in 1890 or 1895.

Similarly, the Orient saw no particular point in distinguishing the incarnation of the Boddhisattva in the third epoch from his incarnation in the second or first epoch. This comparison should not be carried too far, however. For the Easterner the Boddhisattva was always an incarnation of the One. This abstract concentration on the One, this tendency to look for the One, demonstrates the unhistorical nature of Oriental thought; and fundamentally this is equally characteristic of all the unhistorical conceptions of the pre-Christian era. The single exception is the historical point of view that appears in the Old Testament. In the case of the Old Testament this historical viewpoint was only a beginning, which reached a more perfected stage in the New Testament. The important thing here is to look at the whole line of development, as such, and not confine ourselves to looking at what is repeated in the individual cycles, but rather to try to see what constitutes the focus of all development. Then we shall be justified in saying that it is absolute nonsense to say that there *can* be no such focus of development.

This is the point about which the various peoples, scattered across the world, must come to an understanding: the subject of historical development. The first thing they must realize is that for a true and genuine study of mankind it is absolutely vital to take the historical element into consideration. Even today one may have the experience that if a true and genuine Christianity is taken to the East—not a fanatical or denominational Christianity—but a Christianity that wishes to hold its own beside the other Eastern religions, then one may be received with the words, "It is true that you have only the one God who incarnated only once, in Palestine. But we are ahead of you for we have many embodiments of God." For an Oriental such an answer would be a matter of course. It is connected with his special gift for looking always for the recurrence of the One. By contrast, what is important for the Westerner is that everything should have a center of gravity. So if people speak of several incarnations of Christ they are making the same mistake as if they were to say that it is ridiculous to pretend that only one fulcrum is needed for a pair of scales, and that the load on one side is balanced by the weights on the other; and moreover that the pair of scales can be supported in two, three or four places. But this of course is nonsense—a pair of scales can have only one fulcrum. So if we wish to understand evolution as a whole we must look for the one fulcrum, the single center of gravity, and not think it would be better if we looked for successive incarnations of the Christ. Regarding this question the nations and peoples spread across the world will have to come to the understanding that in the course of human history it was necessary for men to come to a historical way of thinking, to a concept of history, as the only conception in a higher sense truly worthy of man.

This manner of looking at human evolution from a historical standpoint came about only very slowly; it began in the most primitive conditions. We find this historical evolution first indicated in the Old Testament through the repeated emphasizing of the nature of the people of the Old

Testament, how they belong to the bloodstream of Abraham, Isaac and Jacob, how the blood flows through successive generations; fundamentally what develops in this people is a form of descent through the blood, of propagation through the blood. As a man progresses through the successive periods in his life and time plays its part in this process, so it is also in the case of the entire people of the Old Testament. And if we examine the process down to its very details we shall find that in truth the sequence of the generations of the Old Testament peoples is analogous to the life of an individual human being insofar as he develops naturally, developing in himself everything that we may think of as being possible through his physical disposition. What could happen as a result of the passing on of his heritage from father to son as an invariable process is described for us in the Old Testament; and it also describes the kind of religious faith that came into being because later generations always clung to those who were their blood relatives. The significance to be attached to the bloodstream in the natural life of the individual human being is made applicable to the entire people of the Old Testament. And just as the soul element, as it were, emerges in individual man at a particular time and plays a specific part in his life, so—and this is an especially interesting fact—does something similar occur in the historical evolution of the Old Testament.

Let us take the case of a child. Here we see that nature predominates; its bodily needs are at first dominant. The soul-element is still concealed within the body; it does not wish to emerge fully. Bodily well-being is produced through pleasant external impressions; unpleasant, painful impressions of the external world are also reflected in the manifestations of the child's soul-nature. Then the child grows up, and through his natural development his soul-element begins to be dominant; we then enter a stage in life—the age varies in different people, but in general this occurs in the twenties—when men give full expression to the element of soul that is within them. Purely bodily pains and necessities recede into the background and the soul configuration emerges in a marked manner. There follows a period during which the soul-element in man is inclined to recede more into the background—and this period will be longer or shorter in different men. It may happen that a man will retain his specific soul-nature his whole life long. Nevertheless something else is really present, even if in his twenties someone persists in emphasizing what he is, as if the world had been only waiting for just that specific soul-element that he bears within him. This is likely to happen especially when a man has strong spiritual potential, as, for example, when he possesses a marked talent for philosophy. It then seems as if the world had only been waiting until he came and established the correct philosophical system, for which only *his* soul configuration was suited. And it may happen that what is right and good may emerge in this way. Then there comes a time when we begin to see what the world may give through others. Then we allow something different to speak through ourselves, and we take up what others have achieved before us.

The whole body of the ancient Hebrew people is presented in the Old Testament as analogous to an individual man. We see how in the time of Abraham, Isaac and Jacob everything in this people develops through its racial characteristics. And if you follow up what has been described here you will say that it was certain racial characteristics that provided the impulses in the Old Testament. Then came the time when this people formed its soul, in the same way that individual man forms his personal soul in his twenties. It is at this point that the prophet Elijah appears, for Elijah seems in himself like the whole soul peculiar to the Hebrew people. After him came the other prophets of whom I spoke a few days ago, telling you that they were the souls of the widely varying initiates of other peoples who came together in the people of the Old Testament. Now the soul of this people listens to what the souls of the other peoples have to say. What Elijah left behind and what the souls of other peoples have to say through their prophets, who now reincarnate in the people of the Old Testament, is blended as in a great harmony or symphony.

Thus did the body of the old Hebrew people come to maturity. Then in a certain way it dies by retaining only the spiritual, what remains spiritual, in its faith and religion, as we see so wonderfully in the picture of the Maccabees. We could say, "Here appears in a picture of the Maccabees the Old Testament people, now grown old, slowly lying down to rest in its old age, yet at the same time proclaiming, through the sons of the Maccabees, its awareness of the eternity of the human soul. The eternity of individual man confronts us as the consciousness of the people. And it seems as though while the body of the people is sinking to its destruction, its soul continues as a soul seed in an entirely new form. Where is this soul to be found?

This Elijah-soul is at the same time the soul of the Old Testament people, as it enters the Baptist and lives in him. When he was imprisoned and then beheaded by Herod, what happened then to his soul? This we have already indicated. His soul left the body and worked on as an aura; and into the domain of this aura Christ Jesus entered. Where then is the soul of Elijah, the soul of John the Baptist? The Mark Gospel indicates this clearly enough. The soul of John the Baptist, of Elijah, becomes the group soul of the Twelve; it lives, and continues to live in the Twelve. We can say that it is artistically and pictorially shown in a remarkable manner how the teaching of Christ Jesus, his way of teaching, differed when he taught the crowd and when he taught his own individual disciples—and this, even before the Mark Gospel has told us of the death of John the Baptist. We have already spoken of this. However, a change takes place when

113

the soul of Elijah is freed from John the Baptist and works on further in the Twelve as a group soul. And this is indicated, for from this time onward—this is quite clear if we read the passage and reread it—Christ makes greater demands on His disciples than before. He calls upon them to understand higher things. And it is very remarkable what He expects them to understand, and what later on He reproaches them for not understanding. Read it in the Gospel just as it is written. I have already referred to one aspect of these events, namely that mention was made of an increase of bread when Elijah went to the widow at Sareptah, and how, when the soul of Elijah was freed from John the Baptist, again an increase of bread is reported. But now Christ Jesus demands of His disciples that they should understand in particular the meaning of this increase of bread. Before that time He had not spoken to them in such terms. Now they ought to understand what was the destiny of John the Baptist after he had been beheaded through Herod, what happened in the case of the feeding of the five thousand when the fragments of bread were collected in twelve baskets, and what happened when the four thousand were fed from seven loaves and the fragments were collected in seven baskets. So He said to them:

> "Do you notice and understand nothing? Are your souls still in the darkness? You have eyes and do not see, ears and do not hear, and you do not think of what I did. I broke the five loaves for the five thousand. How many baskets of the fragments did you gather?" They answered, "Twelve."
> "And when seven loaves were divided among four thousand, how many basketsful of fragments did you gather?" And they answered, "Seven."
> Then he said to them, "Do you still not understand?" (Mark 8: 17–21.)

He reproaches them severely because they cannot understand the meaning of these revelations. Why does He

114

do this? Because the thought was in His mind, "Now that the spirit of Elijah has been freed, he lives in you, and you must gradually prove yourselves worthy of his penetration into your souls, so that you may understand things that are higher than what you have hitherto been able to understand." When Christ Jesus spoke to the crowd, He spoke in parables, in pictures, because there was still in their souls an echo of what had formerly been perceived in the supersensible world in imaginations, in imaginative knowledge. For this reason He had to speak to the crowd in the way used by the old clairvoyants. To those who came out of the Old Testament people and became His disciples He could interpret the parables in a Socratic manner, in accordance with ordinary human reasoning capacities. He could speak to the new sense that had been given to mankind after the old clairvoyance had died out. But because Elijah's spirit as a group soul came near to the Twelve and permeated them like a common aura, they could, or at least it was possible for them to become in a higher sense clairvoyant. Enlightened as they were through the spirit of Elijah-John they could, when the Twelve were united together, perceive what they could not attain as individual men. It was for this that Christ wished to educate them.

To what end did He wish to educate them? Fundamentally what is this story of the increase of bread, the first time the division of five loaves among five thousand and the gathering of twelve basketsful of fragments? Then the second time, when seven loaves were divided among four thousand, with seven basketsful over? This has been a difficult theme for commentators. In our time they have come to an agreement and simply say that the people had brought bread with them, and when they had been made to sit down in rows they unpacked their fragments. Even those who wish to adhere to the letter of the Gospel story seem to have agreed on this interpretation. But when things are taken in this external manner they are reduced to nothing but external trappings and external ceremony; and one cannot tell why the whole story should have been related at all. On the other hand we cannot of course think of black magic, though if a plentiful quantity of bread had really been conjured up out of five or seven loaves respectively then it would indeed have been black magic. But it can neither be a question of black magic, nor yet a process found satisfactory by Philistines who suppose that the people had brought bread with them and unpacked it. Something special is meant by the story. I have indicated this when I interpreted the other Gospels, and in this Gospel it is clearly indicated what is the point at issue:

> And the apostles gathered around Jesus and reported to Him everything they had done and what they had taught. And he said to them: "Withdraw to a solitary place apart and rest for a short time." (Mark 6: 30–31.)

We should pay careful attention to this saying. Christ Jesus sends His apostles away to a solitary place so that they could rest for a while; that is to put themselves into a condition which comes naturally when one goes into solitude. What now do they see? In this different condition what do they see? They are led into a new kind of clairvoyance, which they are able to enter because the spirit of Elijah-John now overshadows them. Until this time Christ has interpreted the parables for them; now He allows a new clairvoyance to come over them. And what do they see? They see in comprehensive pictures the development of humanity, they see how the peoples of the future gradually come near to the Christ Impulse. The disciples see in the spirit what is described here as the multiple increase of bread. It is an act of clairvoyance. And like other such clairvoyant perceptions it flits past if one is not accustomed to it. It is for this reason that the disciples could not understand it for so long.

116

In the lectures that are to follow we shall have to occupy ourselves ever more intensively with the fact, especially evident in the Mark Gospel, that the stories concerned with outer events in the world of the senses pass over little by little into reports of clairvoyant moments and the Gospel is then understandable only through spiritual research. Let us, for example, imagine ourselves in the period just after the beheading of John, and let us suppose ourselves to be affected by the Christ Impulse, which was already in the world. From the point of view of ordinary sense perception Christ first of all seems to us like a lonely personality, unable to achieve much. But a clairvoyant vision, schooled in a modern manner, perceives the element of *time.* Christ did not appear only to those who were living then in Palestine, but to all who will appear in future generations. All of them gather around Him; and what He is able to give to them He gives to thousands upon thousands. This is the way the apostles see Him. They see Him actively working from His own epoch onward through countless millennia, casting His impulse forward spiritually into all perspectives of the future. They perceive how all human beings of the future come near. In this process they are indeed in very special measure united with the Christ.

We must especially recognize that from now on the entire presentation of the Mark Gospel is permeated by the spiritual. How the Gospel grows ever more profound because of this permeation we shall perceive in the lectures that are to follow. But let us focus our attention on one thing —a scene that can be understood only through the spiritual scientific method of research. This scene follows closely on the one we have just quoted:

> And Jesus and his disciples went into the areas around Caesarea Philippi. And on the way he asked his disciples, "What do people say of me? Who do they say I am?"
> So they told him, "Some say you are John the Baptist;

others that you are Elijah, and yet others that you are one of the prophets."

And he asked them, "What about you? Who do you say that I am?"

Peter answered and told him, "You are the Christ."

And he warned them not to tell anyone about him.

And he began to teach then that the Son of Man must suffer much and be rejected by the elders and the chief priests and the scribes; and that he would undergo death and after three days be raised. And he spoke quite openly of the matter.

Then Peter went close to him and began to scold him. But he turned round and when he saw his disciples he scolded Peter in this way. "Get behind me, Satan! You are thinking only of what is convenient for men, not for God." (8: 27–33.)

Surely a tough nut for Gospel commentators to crack! For what does the entire passage really mean? Unless we engage in spiritual research nothing in the passage is comprehensible. Christ asks the disciples, "Who do the people say I am?" And they answer, "Some say you are John the Baptist!" But John the Baptist had been beheaded a short time before, and in any event Christ was already teaching while John was still alive! Could the people have been talking such obvious nonsense when they took Christ for John the Baptist while the Baptist was still living? It might have been still acceptable when they said He was Elijah or another prophet. But then Peter says, "You are the Christ!" That is to say, he reveals something of a sublime nature that could have been spoken only from the holiest part of his being. Then, a few lines later, Christ is supposed to have told him, "Satan, get behind me. You are thinking only of what is convenient for men, not for God." Is it possible for anyone to believe that after Peter had made his sublime affirmation Christ would have insulted him by calling him Satan? Or can one believe what was said just before, that Christ warned them not to tell anyone about Him, that is to say, to tell no one that Peter believes Him to be the Christ? Then the Gospel goes on to say, "He began to teach them that the Son of Man must suffer much, and be rejected and killed, and then after three days be raised. And he spoke quite openly about the matter." Then after Peter scolded Him because of what He had said He calls Peter a "Satan." But most curious of all is the remaining passage where it is said that "Jesus and his disciples went into the areas around Caesarea Philippi," and the rest. The Gospel always tells how they speak to Him, and then later it is said, "and he began to teach them . . ." and so on. But then it says, "But he turned around, and when he saw his disciples he scolded Peter." Earlier it is said that He spoke to them and taught them. Did He do all this with His back turned to them? For it is said that "he turned around and saw his disciples." Did He really turn His back on them and talk into the air?

You see what a tangle of incomprehensible things is to be found in this single passage. We can only marvel that such things are accepted without ever looking for real and truthful explanations. But if you look at the Gospel commentaries they either hurry over such passages or they are interpreted in a most curious way. It is true that there have been some discussions and controversies; but few will claim they have made them any wiser.

At this moment we wish to stick to only one point, and bring before our souls a picture of what has been said. We pointed out that after the death of John the Baptist when the soul of Elijah-John passed over into the disciples as a group soul, then the first true "miracle" was accomplished, and it will become ever clearer how this word is to be understood. Here we come upon a completely incomprehensible passage in which Christ Jesus is portrayed as having said to His disciples, "What do people believe is now happening?" In truth the question can be put also in this way, for what concerned these people most of all was what the source of these actions was, where these happenings came from. To this the disciples reply, "People think it has something to do with—to use a trivial expression—John the Baptist, or it has to do with Elijah or one of the other prophets. And because of this connection the deeds that we have witnessed have taken place."

So Christ Jesus then asks, "But where do *you* believe these things come from?" and now Peter answers, "They come from the fact that you are the Christ." With these words Peter, in the sense of the Mark Gospel, placed himself through this knowledge at the midpoint of the evolution of mankind. For what did he actually say with these words? Let us picture to ourselves what he said.

In former times it was the initiates who were the great leaders of humanity, those who were taken up to the final stage of initiation in the sacred mysteries. It was these men who approached the gate of death, who had been immersed in the elements, had remained for three days outside their bodies and during these three days were in the supersensible worlds. Then they were brought back again into their bodies and became thereafter emissaries, ambassadors from the supersensible worlds. It was always those initiates who had become initiates by means such as these who were the great leaders of mankind. Now Peter says, "You are the Christ," that is, "You are a leader who has not gone through the mysteries in this way but has come down from the cosmos and become a leader of mankind." Something which in all other cases had happened in a different way, through initiation, was now to take place on the earth plane once and for all as a historical fact. It was something colossal that Peter had just proclaimed. So what had he to be told? He had to be told that this was something that must not be brought before the people. It is something that according to the most sacred laws of the past must remain a mystery; it is not permissible to speak of the mysteries. That is what Peter had to be told at that moment.

Yet the whole meaning of the further evolution of humanity is that with the Mystery of Golgotha something that otherwise took place only in the depths of the mysteries had now been manifested on the plane of world history. Through what happened on Golgotha, the lying in the grave for three days, the resurrection, through this what otherwise had taken place only in the depths and darkness of the mysteries was placed historically on the earth plane. In other words, the moment in time had now come when what had hitherto been regarded as a sacred law: that silence must be preserved about the mysteries, must be broken. The law that one has to be silent about the mysteries had been established by men. But now, through the Mystery of Golgotha, the mysteries must become manifest! Within the soul of the Christ a decision was taken, the greatest world-historical decision, when He resolved that what until now had always, according to human law, been kept secret must now be made manifest before the sight of all, before world history.

Let us think of this moment in world history when the Christ meditated and reflected in this way, "I am looking at the whole development of mankind. The laws of mankind forbid me to speak about death and resurrection, about raising from the dead, and about the sacred mystery of initiation. Yet no! I have in truth been sent down to the earth by the Gods to make these things manifest. It is not for me to conform to what people say, but I must act in conformity with what the Gods tell me." It is in this moment that the decision to make the mysteries manifest is prepared. And Christ must shake off the irresolution that might arise from a wish to maintain within human evolution what human commands have enjoined. "Get behind me, irresolution, and decision, grow in me, the decision to place before all

121

mankind what hitherto has been kept in the depths of the mysteries.'' Christ addresses His own resolution after He had rejected everything that could make Him irresolute when He says, ''Get behind me,'' and at this moment He resolves to fulfill what He had been sent down to earth by God to accomplish.

In this passage we have to do with the greatest monologue in world history, the greatest that has ever taken place in the whole of earth evolution, the monologue of a God about making manifest the mysteries. No wonder that the God's monologue is from the beginning incomprehensible to the human intellect. If we wish to penetrate into its depths we must wish, at least in some measure, to make ourselves worthy of understanding the God's monologue through which the deed of the God moves one step further towards realization. More of this tomorrow.

LECTURE 7

When we are engaged in the study of one or other of the Gospels and trying to explain it, it would doubtless be best to leave the other Gospels altogether out of account. By this means it would be possible to reach the purest and best understanding of the prevailing tone of each. But it is obvious that such an approach could lead to misunderstandings, unless a ray of light were thrown upon it from one of the other Gospels. And precisely what we called yesterday the "greatest monologue in world history" can easily be misunderstood if someone were to consult in a superficial and not too accurate manner what had, for example, to be said in connection with the similar passage in the Matthew Gospel in the lectures I gave in Bern. Indeed, an objection made from such a standpoint would really in a deeper logical sense be the same as if the statement were made that a man once stood on this platform and on his left was a bouquet of roses. Then another statement would be made that a man once stood on this platform and on his right was a bouquet of roses, and a man who had not been present proceeded to object, saying that there must be a mistake since one time the bouquet of roses was on the right and the other time on the left. It all depends on where the observer in question was standing, for both statements can be correct. So it is with the Gospels, where we are not concerned simply with an abstract biography of Christ Jesus, but with a rich world of external and occult facts that are presented in them.

In order to picture to ourselves this viewpoint let us now consider again what we called yesterday the "greatest monologue in world history," the soliloquy of the God. We must recognize that the whole episode was especially concerned with the relationship between Christ Jesus and His closest disciples. And we must include in such a study most particularly what was said yesterday, that the spirit of Elijah, after it had been freed from the physical body of John the Baptist, was actually active as a kind of group soul of the disciples. What happened then cannot just be related in a simple external way since it took place in a much more complicated manner. To a certain extent there was a deep and inner connection between the soul of the Christ and the souls of the Twelve. Everything that took place within the soul of Christ was made up of processes of significance for that time, rich and manifold processes. But all that took place in the soul of Christ took place again in a kind of reflected image, a reflection in the souls of the disciples, but divided into twelve parts. In this way each of the Twelve experienced, as in a reflected image, a part of what happened in the soul of Christ Jesus; but each of the Twelve experienced it somewhat differently. What took place within the soul of Christ Jesus was like a harmony, a great symphony, reflected in the souls of each of the Twelve, in much the same way as twelve instruments can give forth a harmony. So any event that concerns one or more of the disciples in particular may be described from two sides. It is possible to describe how the event in question appeared within the soul of Christ, as, for example, in the case of the great world-historical monologue of Christ Jesus. It is possible to describe how it was experienced within His soul, and then it appears as it was described yesterday. But it also takes place in a certain reflected image in the soul of Peter. Peter has the same soul experience. But, whereas in the case of Christ Jesus it encompasses the whole of mankind, Peter's identical experience encompasses only a twelfth part of all mankind, a twelfth, a single zodiacal sign of the entire Christ spirit. For

124

this reason it must be pictured differently when it concerns Christ Jesus Himself.

It must be spoken of in this way if we are to describe it in the sense of the Mark Gospel, for most remarkable things are described in it, and especially what is presented as having taken place within the soul of Christ Jesus Himself. By contrast the Matthew Gospel pictures more what has reference to the soul of Peter, and what Christ Jesus added to explain what took place within Peter's soul. If you read the Gospel carefully, you will notice how in the Matthew Gospel certain words have been added which give us the picture as perceived from the side of Peter. Otherwise, why should the words have been added, "Blessed are you, Simon, son of Jonah, for flesh and blood have not revealed it to you but my Father in the heavens." (Matt. 16: 17)? In other words the soul of Peter felt something of what the soul of Christ had been feeling. But while Peter's soul felt that his master was Christ, this should be understood as meaning that Peter was for a time raised upward to an experience in his higher "I," and that he was overwhelmed by this experience and then fell back, as it were, afterward. Nevertheless it was possible for him to penetrate through to a knowledge which, with a different aim and purpose, came about within the soul of Christ. Because Peter was able to do this, there followed the handing over of the power of the keys mentioned in the Matthew Gospel (Matt. 16: 19), about which we spoke in our interpretation of that Gospel. By contrast, in speaking of the Mark Gospel we have emphasized, forcefully and simply, those words that indicate that the event, quite apart from what happened within Peter, took place at the same time and in a parallel manner as the monologue of God.

This is how we must look at these things, enabling us to feel how Christ Jesus deals with His own, how He leads them on from stage to stage, and how after the spirit of Elijah-John had passed over into them He could lead them more deeply than He could earlier into the comprehension of spiritual secrets. And one of our first impressions is that it is significant that the passage we discussed at the end of our last lecture, the monologue of the God, should be closely followed by the so-called Transfiguration or Transformation scene. That is also a significant element in the dramatic composition of the Mark Gospel. In order to shed light on the Transfiguration we need to point out a few facts that are related to many things necessary for the understanding of the picture presented in the Gospels. Let us begin by referring to one of these.

You can read often in the Mark Gospel, as well as in the other Gospels, how Christ Jesus speaks of how the Son of Man must suffer many things, that He would be set upon by the scribes and high priests, that He would be put to death and after three days would be raised. You will notice how up to a certain point the apostles are unable to understand at first what is meant by the suffering, death and raising of the Son of Man, how they experience a real difficulty particularly in understanding this passage (Mark 9: 31–32). Why are we confronted with this peculiar fact? Why is it precisely with reference to the understanding of the Mystery of Golgotha itself that the apostles experience these difficulties? What then *is* the Mystery of Golgotha? We have already spoken of this. It is nothing else but the drawing forth of initiation from the depths of the mysteries onto the plane of world history. Of course there is a crucial difference between the average initiation and the Mystery of Golgotha. This difference consists in the following.

All those who were initiated into the mysteries of the various peoples had in a certain sense experienced the same thing. An initiate was made to suffer, and one could say that he was apparently dead for three days, during which his

126

spirit remained in the spiritual worlds outside his body. Then his spirit was brought back into his body in such a way that the spirit in his body could remember what it had undergone in the spiritual world, and could then appear as a messenger, proclaiming the secrets of the spiritual world. Thus we can say that initiation is a journey into death, though in such a death the spirit is not separated entirely from the body, but only for a limited time. Initiation involves remaining outside the physical body and returning into it, thereby becoming a messenger for the secrets of the divine world. It took place after careful preparation, and after the candidate had reached a condition where his soul forces were so concentrated within him that he could live without using the instrument of his physical body. Then after these three and a half days he had to unite himself again with his physical body. We may say that the initiate passed through this by withdrawing into a higher world unconnected with ordinary historical events.

Although the Mystery of Golgotha was, to outward appearance, similar, it differed in its inner nature. The events that occurred during the period when the Christ dwelt in the body of Jesus of Nazareth had actually resulted in the genuine physical death of the physical body of Jesus of Nazareth. The spirit of Christ remained for three days outside the physical body but it then returned. And now it was not in the physical body but in the concentrated etheric body, concentrated in such a way that it was possible for the disciples to perceive it, as described in the Gospels—with the consequence that Christ could walk and become visible also after the event of Golgotha. Thereby initiation, which formerly took place in the depths of the mysteries, hidden from external eyes, was presented as a historical event, a unique event, before all mankind. Through this, initiation was, in a sense, lifted out of the mysteries; it had been accomplished by the one Christ before the eyes of everyone.

And precisely with this event the ancient world came to an end and the new era began.

From the picture that has been given you of the prophets you have seen that the prophetic spirit, and what was given by this prophetic spirit to the ancient Hebrew people, differed from the spirit of initiation prevalent among other peoples. These other peoples had their initiates, who were initiated in the manner we have just described. This was not the case with the ancient Hebrew people. With them it was not a question of initiation of the same kind as among the other peoples. Here we have to do with an elemental emergence of the spirit within the bodies of those who appeared as prophets; something resembling "geniuses of spirituality" appeared. To enable this to happen we see that in the middle prophetic period souls appear in the ancient Hebrew people who in earlier incarnations had been initiates among the other peoples, so that they experience everything they give to the ancient Hebrew people as a memory of what they themselves had received in their initiation. For this reason spiritual life did not shine into the ancient Hebrew people in the same way as it did into other peoples. In the case of these other peoples it occurred through an act, through initiation, whereas in the case of the Old Testament people it came by virtue of the gifts that had been implanted in those who worked actively as prophets among the people. Through the activity of their prophets the Hebrew people were made ready to experience that unique initiation which was no longer that of a human individuality but of a cosmic individuality, if, indeed one may speak of an initiation at all in this case, which is no longer correct. Through this the Hebrew people were prepared to receive something that was to take the place of the old initiation: they were made ready to view the Mystery of Golgotha in the right way. But one consequence of this was that the apostles, who belonged to the Old Testament people, had at first no understanding of the words that characterize initiation. Christ Jesus spoke about initiation when He expressed himself in such terms as hastening toward death, remaining in the grave for three days and being raised from the dead. This is a description of initiation. If He had described it in a different way they would have understood Him. But because such a way of speaking of initiation was foreign to the Old Testament people the Twelve could not at first understand His description. So it is quite correctly pointed out to us that the disciples were astonished and did not know to what He was referring when He spoke of the suffering and death and raising of the Son of Man.

Such things are therefore entirely in accord with the spiritual content of the events as they are historically presented. When the ancient initiate experienced his initiation it is true that he was in a higher world while he was outside his body; he was not in the ordinary sense-perceptible world. We may say that while he was outside his body he was at one with the realities of a higher plane. While he was free of his body in the spiritual world, returning later to his body, what had he experienced? It was memory. He had to speak in such a way that he could say, "I remember my experiences when I was free of my body, in the same way as in ordinary life one can remember what one experienced yesterday or the day before." He could bear witness to them. As far as these initiates are concerned it did not amount to much more than that they bore in their souls the secrets of the spiritual worlds in the same way that the human soul retains in memory what it experienced yesterday. And as the soul is united with what it retains as memory, so the initiates were united with the secrets of the spiritual world that they carried within themselves.

What was the reason for this? It was because before the Mystery of Golgotha human souls on earth were not adapted to allowing the kingdoms of the heavens, the supersensible worlds, to penetrate into the ego. They could not approach the true ego, could not unite themselves with it. Only if a man could see beyond himself or could glimpse the divine by means of the clairvoyance that existed in those ancient times, if, as I might put it, he dreamt himself away or were freed from his ego through initiation, could he enter the supersensible worlds. But within the ego there was no comprehension, no understanding of the higher worlds. This is how it was in those ancient times. Before the Mystery of Golgotha man could not unite himself with the spiritual worlds even by making use of all the forces pertaining to his ego.

The secret that was to be revealed to the people through the baptism of John was that the time had now come near when the kingdoms of heaven were to shine right into the ego; they were to approach the ego, the earthly ego. In truth it has been indicated all through the ages how what man could experience as his soul element could not in ancient times enter the supersensible worlds. In ancient times there was something like a disharmony between the way in which the true home of man, the spiritual world, was experienced, and that which, if we wish to describe the old soul nature as "ego," was active in the inner being of man. This human inner self was separated from the spiritual world, and only in exceptional conditions could it be united with it. And when all the might of what was later to become the ego and to live within man, when all the power and the impulses of the ego filled him, for example through initiation, or through remembering the experience of initiation in a former incarnation in a later one—when the power and might of the ego prematurely penetrated into his bodily nature, what happened then? It has always been pointed out that in the pre-Christian era the ego force, too powerful for the human bodily nature, could find its proper place in the body, and broke through what was destined for the ego.

For this reason those human beings who bear within

themselves more of the supersensible world, bearing within themselves in pre-Christian times something of what would in a later age become the ego, such persons split apart their human bodily constitution with this ego force because this force is too strong for the pre-Christian era. This is clearly alluded to, for example, in the case of certain individualities during a particular incarnation who possess this ego force in themselves, but this ego can remain within them only because the body is in some way wounded, or vulnerable, wounded and having a vulnerable spot. It is in this spot that the individuality is exposed to danger from his surroundings more than in any other part of his body. We need only recall the vulnerability of Achilles' heel, of Siegfried and Oedipus whose bodies are split asunder by the force of the ego. These examples of wounds demonstrate to us how only a damaged body is compatible with the greatness of the ego, and the superhuman ego force that is within it.

Perhaps the significance of what I am trying to place before our souls could be grasped better if I formulate it in a different way. Let us suppose that someone in pre-Christian times were to be filled, not necessarily consciously, with all those impulses and forces that later on will penetrate the ego, and that these forces which I might call a superego force, a superhuman force, were to dive down into his body. He would have to break apart his body and not perceive it as it was when it had its weak ego, its weak inner self, within it. A man of olden times would necessarily have seen it differently if he possessed within himself the whole power of the ego, enabling him to rise up out of his body. He would have seen the body as it actually was, broken under the influence of the superego. He would have seen it with every kind of wound imaginable because in ancient times only a weak ego, a weak inner self, penetrated the body so slightly that it could remain whole.

What I have just said was indeed stated by the prophets.

The passage (Zechariah 12: 10) is so formulated that it runs approximately as follows, "A man who unites in himself the full force of egohood and is confronted with the human body, sees it wounded, pierced through with holes. For the higher ego force which in ancient times could not yet live within the inner self, pierces through, penetrates and makes holes in the body." This is an impulse that runs through the evolution and development of mankind for the reason that as a result of the influence of Lucifer and Ahriman in pre-Christian times only a portion of the ego could be bestowed on man. And because the body is adapted only to the smaller portion and not to the whole force of the ego, it is worn down. It was not because this took place in the pre-Christian era but because in the case of Christ Jesus the full power of the ego entered all at once, and entered with the utmost strength into His bodily being, that this body had to appear not only with a single wound, as was the case with so many human individualities who carried a superego, but with *five wounds*. These were necessary because the Christ-Being, that is, the full ego of man, projected far beyond the bodily form appropriate for those times. It was for this reason that the cross had to be erected on the physical plane of world history, that cross that bore the body of Christ, a human body such as that of man would be if for a moment the whole of man's nature, a large part of which has been lost through the influence of Lucifer and Ahriman, were to live within one single human being.

It is a profound mystery that is given to us by occult science in the picture of the Mystery of Golgotha. Anyone who understands the true nature of the human being and of humanity, and the nature of the earthly ego and its relation to the form of the human body, knows that when the human body is entirely penetrated by the earthly ego such a penetration would be abnormal for the ordinary man as he walks about on earth. But when a man goes out of himself and sees himself from outside and is able to ask the question, "How would this body be if the totality of egohood were to enter into it?" then his answer must be that it would be pierced by five wounds. The form of the cross on Golgotha with Christ upon it with His wounds is derived from the nature of man and from the very being of the earth itself. From our study of the nature of man it is possible for the picture of the Mystery of Golgotha to arise for us out of our own knowledge. Strange as it may seem, it is actually possible to see how the cross is raised on Golgotha, how the crucifixion takes place, and to perceive directly the truth of this historical event, and all this without the use of clairvoyance when such a vision would be natural. Because of the Mystery of Golgotha it is possible for the human intellect to approach so closely to this mystery that if it is used with sufficient sharpness and subtlety it can be transformed into an imagination, into a picture that then contains the truth. If we understand the nature of Christ and His relation to the human bodily form, our imagination can be guided in this way in such a manner that the picture of Golgotha itself arises for us. The older Christian painters were often guided in this way. Even though they were not perhaps in all cases clairvoyant, their knowledge of the Mystery of Golgotha was so powerful that it impelled them so far that they were able to picture it in such a way that they could paint it. It was just at this great turning point of human evolution that the understanding of the being of Christ, in other words, the primal ego of man, emerged out of clairvoyance and rose up into the ego-soul of man.

It is possible to see the Mystery of Golgotha through clairvoyance outside the body. By what means? If while within the body a relationship has been established to the Mystery of Golgotha, it is possible also today to perceive it in the higher worlds, and in so doing to receive a full confirmation of the truth of this great nodal point in the evolution

133

of mankind. It is, however, also possible to comprehend the Mystery of Golgotha, and the words I have just spoken ought to make this understanding possible. It is, of course, necessary to reflect and meditate on them for a long time. If anyone should feel it difficult to grasp what has just been said, such a feeling is perfectly justifiable, for it goes without saying that anything that can lead the human soul to a full understanding of the highest and most significant event that has ever happened on earth is bound to be difficult. In a certain way the disciples had to be led toward this understanding; and of all those who had to be led gradually to a new understanding of the evolution of mankind, Peter, James, and John proved to be the most suitable.

It is good for us to picture to ourselves from as many sides as we can the significant epoch that began at the time of the Mystery of Golgotha. Therefore it was especially helpful that you were able to hear this morning how Hegel envisaged this turning point of time. We need everything that human understanding can contribute if we are to grasp the significance of what entered into human evolution at that time, something that had been maturing during the preceding centuries and took place about the time of the Mystery of Golgotha, thereafter slowly preparing and conditioning the further evolution of humanity. It manifested itself in various parts of the earth and we can trace it not only in Palestine where the Mystery of Golgotha itself occurred, but in other parts of the earth where the Mystery of Golgotha did *not* occur. If we proceed in the right way we can trace how as a result of the Mystery of Golgotha mankind descended and then reascended, and was uplifted as the Mystery of Golgotha spread throughout the Western world. In particular we can trace the descent of mankind, and this indeed is especially interesting.

Let us consider once again the land of Greece, and picture to ourselves what happened there half a millennium before the Mystery of Golgotha. In the East, where Krishna appeared, people were in a certain way ahead of their time in the period when the old clairvoyance was dying out. Indeed, there was something remarkable about the culture of ancient India. During the time immediately following the Atlantean age with the great cultural flowering of the first post-Atlantean epoch, the human soul still had the possibility of seeing into the spiritual world in the purest manner. In the case of the Rishis this faculty was accompanied by the wonderful ability to present what they had seen in such a way that it could influence later ages. Then when the clairvoyance disappeared, what they had given could be preserved in such significant revelations as those given out by Krishna; although the true clairvoyance already had been extinguished by the end of the third epoch. But what had been perceived in this earlier age was preserved in wonderful words through Krishna and his pupils, with the result that what at an earlier time had been seen could now be expressed in writing. So what happened further west, for example in Greece, never happened in India at all.

If we perceive correctly the Indian world we may say that the old clairvoyance died out, and because it died out some men, among whom Krishna was the most important, wrote down in wonderful words what had formerly been seen. This, then, appears in the Vedas, in the word; and anyone who immerses himself in the word experiences an echo of it in his soul. But this is quite different from what came forth, for example, in Socrates or other philosophers. What may be called Western intellect, Western power of judgment, never appears in Indian souls. Nor can there be found one example in India of what we today speak of in the fullest sense as the inborn power of the ego. As a result just as the old clairvoyance was dying out there came an urge toward Yoga, a new means of ascending into the spiritual worlds through training as a compensation for the loss of

135

natural clairvoyance. Yoga therefore became an artificial clairvoyance, and the philosophy of Yoga appeared without a time interval, such as that during which, in Greece, for example, a rational philosophy appeared. Nothing of this appeared in India; an interim phase was totally lacking. If we take up the Vedanta philosophy of Vyasa we may say that it is not distinguished for its ideas and intellect as are the teachings of the Western world conceptions, but it appears to have been brought down from higher worlds though expressed in human speech. What is remarkable about it is that it was not achieved through human thinking, nor is it thought out like the characteristic teachings of Socrates and Plato. It was, indeed, the product of clairvoyant perception.

It is difficult to come to a clear idea about such matters. Nevertheless, there is a possibility even at the present time to experience the difference between these two kinds of philosophy. Take up any book on philosophy, any presentation of some Western philosophical system. How has anything that can be regarded as a serious philosophy been achieved? If you could see into the workroom of anyone who can be regarded today as a serious philosopher you would see how it is through the power of logical thinking and logical judgment that such systems are created, and each is built up step by step. But those who work out their philosophies in this way are quite unable to understand that their kind of conceptual weaving can also to a certain extent be perceived clairvoyantly, that a clairvoyant can see it in front of him through his clairvoyance. If therefore, instead of passing through all the individual stages of thought we were to survey clairvoyantly, in one fell swoop so to speak, a number of philosophical theses that have been woven together by the sweat of one's brow, concept by concept, then we shall experience much difficulty in making ourselves understood. Yet the concepts of the Vedanta philosophy are concepts of this kind, and they were seen clairvoyantly. They were not acquired by the sweat of the brow, like the concepts of European philosophers, but were brought down clairvoyantly. They are just the last remnants of the ancient clairvoyance, diluted into abstract concepts. Or else they are the first fragile conquests of Yoga in the supersensible worlds.

Those people who lived more to the West went through different experiences. There we see remarkable and important inner events in the evolution of mankind. Let us take the case of a remarkable philosopher of the sixth century before the Christian era, Pherecydes of Syros. He was indeed a remarkable philosopher, though present-day philosophers do not count him even as a philosopher at all. There are books on philosophy which actually say—I will quote a few words verbatim—that all he gives are childish symbols, childish descriptions. So does a man today speak who imagines himself to be greatly superior to those ancient philosophers. He calls these notions "childish and ingenious." Nevertheless, half a millennium before the Christian era a remarkable thinker emerged in Syros. Certainly he describes things differently from other thinkers, who were later to be called philosophers. For example, Pherecydes says, "Underlying everything visible in the world is a trinity: Chronos, Zeus and Chthon. From Chronos comes the airy, the fiery and the watery element. Ophioneus, a kind of serpent being, comes into conflict with all that stems from these three powers." Even if we have no clairvoyance but only some imagination it is possible to see in front of us everything that he describes. Chronos is put forward not merely as abstract passing time but as a real being in a perceptible form. It is the same with Zeus, the limitless ether, as a living self-perpetuating being; while Chthon, who draws down to earth what once was heavenly, draws together into the planet earth all that is woven in space, in order to make earthly existence possible. All this happens on earth. Then a kind of serpent being interferes, and introduces, so to speak, a hostile element. If we examine what this remarkable Pherecydes of Syros describes, it can easily be understood without the aid of spiritual research. He is a last straggler endowed with the clairvoyance of earlier times. He sees behind the sense world to the real causes, and these he describes with the aid of his clairvoyance. Naturally this does not at all please those who prefer to juggle concepts. He sees the living weaving of the good gods and how hostile powers interfere in their work; and all this he describes from the viewpoint of a clairvoyant. He sees how the elements are born out of Chronos, out of Time seen as a real being.

So we have in this philosopher Pherecydes of Syros a man who still sees into the world with his soul, gazing into the world disclosed by clairvoyant consciousness, and describing it; and we are able to follow his description. Thus he stands before us in the Western world as late as the sixth century, B.C. while Thales, Anaximenes, Anaximander and Heraclitus, who are almost his contemporaries, stand there in a quite different manner. Here two worlds actually come together. But how does it appear within the souls of these men? The old clairvoyance has been extinguished, paralyzed in them, and at most all that is left is a longing for the spiritual worlds. What, then, do they experience in place of the living vision that the sage of Syros still possessed, a man who could still look into the world of primal causes? This world has closed to them; they can no longer see into it. It is as if this world wished to close itself to them, as if it was still half present for them but nevertheless eluded them, with the result that they replace the old clairvoyance with abstract concepts that belong to the ego. This is how it appears in the souls of these men. Indeed within these Western souls there was a very remarkable condition of soul at that time. It is moving in the direction of intellect and judgment, which are precisely the characteristics of the ego. We see this within individual souls, as, for instance, in Heraclitus who still describes the living weaving fire as the cause of everything, with, we could say, a last trace of true clairvoyant vision. Thales spoke of water, but he did not mean physical, material water any more than Heraclitus meant physical material fire. But it remains something from the elemental world, which they can still half see through while at the same time it half eludes them, so that all they can give out are abstract concepts. In looking into these souls we can understand how something of the soul mood of these men can still echo into our own time.

If only our contemporaries were not so prone to skim thoughtlessly over so much that is of value! It is so easy to skim lightly over a passage in Nietzsche that can profoundly move us, take possession of us and shake our souls. The passage occurs in his posthumous work *Philosophy in the Tragic Age of the Greeks*, where he describes Thales, Anaximander, Heraclitus, Parmenides, Anaxagoras and Empedocles. Right at the beginning of this work there is a passage where, if we truly enter into it, we can see that Nietzsche perceived something of what these first lonely Greek thinkers experienced in their souls. Look up the passage in Nietzsche where he says, "How must it have been with the souls of those heroes of philosophy who had to make the transition from the period of living vision (of which Nietzsche knew nothing but that he was able to sense) to an age when what had formerly been alive in their souls was superseded by dry, abstract, prosaic concepts; when 'being,' that cold, abstract, prosaic notion, appeared, as a 'concept,' replacing the full aliveness of clairvoyant consciousness?" And Neitzsche feels, "It is as if our blood would freeze in our veins when we cross over from the realm of life into the world of concepts in Thales or Heraclitus who use such concepts as 'being' and 'becoming,' so that we pass from the warm realm of becoming over into the icy region of 'concepts.' "

139

We must transport ourselves in feeling into the age in which these men were living, and how they stood when the Mystery of Golgotha was approaching. We must enter into their being in such a way that we can perceive how there is still within them a dim echo of former times, yet how they must content themselves with the power of abstract judgment that lives in the human ego, a power that was unnecessary in earlier times. And whereas in later eras the world of concepts became richer and richer, in the first period when the world of concepts was coming closer the Greek philosophers could grasp nothing but the most simple of them. How they tormented themselves with such concepts as abstract "being," especially the philosophers of the Eleatic school! But it was in this way that the present-day abstract qualities of the ego were prepared.

Let us now think of a soul which is rooted in the West, prepared for the mission of the West, and yet bears within itself the powerful echo of ancient clairvoyance. In India these echoes have long since died away, but they are still present in the West. The soul has the impulse to enter the elemental world, but it is prevented by its consciousness. A mood such as that of the Buddha could not arise in such souls. The Buddha mood would have said, "We are brought into the world of suffering. Let us free ourselves from it." But Western souls wanted to take hold of what was ahead of them. They could not go back into what lay behind them. But in the world in front of them they could find only cold, icy concepts. Consider such a soul as Pherecydes of Syros who was the last to be able to see into the elemental world. Now let us think of one of the other souls who cannot see how the elements are born in a living way out of Chronos. It is unable to see how Ophioneus, the serpent-being, enters into conflict with the higher gods, but it is able to glimpse that something is at work in the physical material world. It cannot see through to Chronos, but it sees the imprint of

Chronos in the world of sense, in fire, water, air and earth. It is not able to see how the higher gods are opposed by the lower gods, and how Lucifer, the serpent-god, rebels; but it does see how harmony and disharmony, friendship and enmity prevail. It sees love and hate as abstract concepts, and fire, water, air, and earth as abstract elements. The soul beholds all that still at that time penetrated into it, but what had been seen earlier by contemporaries is now hidden.

Let us think of such a soul still standing within the livingness of the earlier era, but unable to see into the spiritual world, able only to grasp its external counterpart, a soul which because of its special mission found that what had previously brought bliss to human beings was hidden from it. Yet this soul has nothing from the new world of the ego save a few concepts to which it feels obliged to cling. What we have before us is the soul of Empedocles. If we wish to comprehend the inner being of such a soul, then it is the soul of Empedocles that stands before us. Empedocles is almost a contemporary of the sage of Syros; he lives scarcely two-thirds of a century later. But his soul is constituted quite differently. It had the task of crossing the Rubicon that separated the old clairvoyance from the abstract comprehension of the ego. We see here two worlds suddenly clashing with one another. Here we see the dawning of the ego and how it advances toward its fulfillment. We see the souls of the ancient Greek philosophers who were the first to be condemned to take up what we now call intellect and logic; and we see at the same time how their souls were emptied of the old revelations. Into these souls the new impulse, the impulse of Golgotha, had to be poured.

Thus were their souls constituted when the new impulse was born. But they had to yearn for a new fulfillment; without such a yearning they could not understand it. In Indian thinking there is scarcely any transition comparable with what we find in the lonely Greek thinkers. Therefore Indian philosophy which had just made its transition to the teaching of Yoga hardly offers any possibility of discovering the transition to the Mystery of Golgotha. Greek philosophy was prepared in such a way that it thirsted for the Mystery of Golgotha. Consider the Gnosis, and how it longed in its philosophy for the Mystery of Golgotha. The philosophy of the Mystery of Golgotha rests on a Greek foundation because the best of the Greek souls longed to receive into themselves the impulse of Golgotha.

In order to understand what happened in mankind's evolution we must have good will. We might then be able to perceive something that might be described as a call, and an answering call from the very soil of the earth. If we look at Greece and then further toward Sicily and look into such souls, among whom Empedocles is one of the most outstanding, then we become aware of an astonishing kind of appeal. How can we characterize this for ourselves? What are such souls saying? If we look into the soul of Empedocles we hear something like this, "I know of initiation through history. From history I know that the supersensible world entered into human souls through initiation. Initiation can no longer come alive in us. Now we are living in a different phase of evolution, and we have need of a new impulse that reaches into the ego. Tell me, Impulse, where are you, you who are to take the place of the initiation of the past that we are no longer able to experience, whose task is to place before the new ego the same mystery that was once contained within the old clairvoyance?"

To this appeal there came in answer the cry from Golgotha, "By obeying the gods and not human beings I was permitted to bring down the mysteries and set them before all mankind, so that what could hitherto be found only in the depths of the mysteries might now be bestowed on all mankind."

What was born in Greek souls in southern Europe comes to us as a request from the Western world for a new solution of the world riddle. And as the answer, an answer that can be understood only in the West, comes the great monologue of the God, of which we spoke at the conclusion of yesterday's lecture, and of which we shall speak again tomorrow.

LECTURE 8

In the Gospel of St. Mark directly after the great world-historical monologue which I have described there follows, as you know, the scene known as the Transfiguration or Transformation. I have often pointed out before that for the three disciples who had been taken to the "mountain" on which the Transfiguration took place, this was a kind of higher initiation. At this moment they were to be initiated, as it were, more profoundly into the secrets that were to be entrusted to them, one by one, to enable them to become leaders and guides of mankind. From what we have said before on several occasions we know that this scene contains a series of secrets. Both in the Gospels and other occult writings whenever the "mountain" is spoken of, then we have to do with something occult. In an occult connection it always means when the mountain is spoken of that those who are led to the mountain are led into certain secrets of existence. In the case of the Mark Gospel we feel this especially strongly for a reason that will become apparent if the Gospel is read rightly. But it must be read rightly.

Take, for example, the third chapter of Mark from the 7th to the 23rd or 24th verse. Actually we need not go further than the 22nd verse, but it is necessary to read it with perceptive understanding. Then something will be noticed. It has often been stressed that the expressions "accompany to the mountain" and "leading to the mountain" have an occult meaning. But in this particular chapter we find a threefold activity, and not only an "accompanying to the mountain." If we examine carefully the three passages indicated by Mark, we notice first in verse 7, "And Jesus

144

withdrew with his disciples to the lake," etc. Then, in the 13th verse it is said, "And he went up to the mountain and called to him those who were acceptable to him." Then in verses 20 and 21 we read, "And then he went to his home. And the crowd gathered again so that they could not so much as eat bread. And when his family heard of it they went out to seize him, for they said 'he is out of his mind.' " Thus we are referred to three separate localities, the lake, the mountain and the house. Just as in an occult sense the mountain signifies that something important takes place, so is this also true in the other two cases. In occult writings if such expressions as "being led to the mountain," or "being led to a house," occur, this invariably means that they have an occult significance. When this is the meaning intended in the Gospels some specific circumstance is connected with it. You should remember that it is not only in the Mark Gospel but also in the others that a special revelation or special manifestation is connected especially with the "lake," as when the disciples cross the lake and Christ appears to them. They at first take Him for a ghost, but then become aware that it is He in reality that is approaching them (6: 45–52). And elsewhere you can also find a similar mention in the Gospels of some event that takes place because of the lake, or by the lake. On the mountain he first appoints the Twelve, that is, he confers their occult mission on them. That was an act of occult education. It is again on the mountain that the occult Transfiguration takes place. When he was "at his home," he is declared by his family to be "out of his mind." This was the third thing, and all three are of the greatest and most comprehensive significance.

If we wish to understand what "by the lake" means in this connection we must call to mind something that we have often explained. We have pictured to you how the so-called Atlantean age preceded our post-Atlantean earth period, and that in that age the air was still permeated by dense

145

masses of mist. In the same way that in the Atlantean age human beings possessed the ancient clairvoyance, their way of perceiving and their soul life were quite different because they lived in quite different physical conditions. This was linked to the fact that the physical body was entirely different, since it was embedded in the masses of mist. From this epoch something like an ancient heritage has remained with mankind. If someone in the post-Atlantean age is initiated by some means into occult matters, or comes near to them as was the case with Jesus' disciples, he becomes much more sensitive, more intensely sensitive to his environment and to the natural world around him. As man is today, we might say that, with his robust relationship with the natural world, it is more or less immaterial whether he crosses the sea or stays by the lake, or whether he climbs a mountain— we shall soon see what that means—or whether he is in his own home. How his eyes see and his mind functions do not depend very much on where he happens to be. But when a man acquires a subtler vision and ascends into spiritual cosmic conditions, then it becomes evident how crudely organized his ordinary being is.

If a man, in the time when the old clairvoyance was active, crossed the sea where circumstances were quite different, even if he lived by the coast, his clairvoyant consciousness would be quite differently attuned than if he were on the plain. The greatest exertion, one might say, is necessary to bring forth any clairvoyant forces at all. The lake allows them to be brought forth more easily, but only those forces which are related to something entirely specific, not to everything. For there is again a difference whether clairvoyant consciousness is active on the plain, or whether it is active on the mountaintop. On the heights the sensitive clairvoyant consciousness is again attuned to things quite different from those on the plain. And the results of clairvoyant consciousness are again different if one is by the lake from what they are on the mountain. In each case the distinction must be made.

Of course it is also possible to arouse clairvoyance in a town, but this needs exceptional forces, whereas what we are talking about at present is valid especially for clairvoyance that comes more or less of its own accord. By the lake, by the water, and in masses of mist, the clairvoyant consciousness is especially disposed to perceive *imaginations*, all kinds of things through imagination, and to make use of what has already been acquired. On the mountain, in the rarified air where the proportion of nitrogen and oxygen is differently distributed, clairvoyant consciousness is more attuned to receiving *inspirations*, allowing something new to arise through clairvoyance. Hence the expression "to ascend the mountain" is not meant only symbolically but is used because the conditions obtaining on the mountain favor the possibility of developing new occult powers in oneself. Likewise the expression "to go to the lake" is not meant symbolically, but was chosen because coming in contact with the lake favors imaginative vision and the use of occult powers.

If one is at home, in one's own house, whether one is alone or with relatives, it is most difficult to make use of occult forces. For while it is comparatively easy for a person who has lived for a long time by a lake to believe—as long as conditions are favorable—that he experiences imaginations through the veil of his corporeality, and easier still for a person who lives in the mountains to believe that he is ascending higher, in the case of a person who is at home, one can feel only that he is outside his body, "out of his mind." This is not to say that he could not develop occult powers, but only that this does not seem to be in harmony with his surroundings. It is less natural than it would be if he were by a lake, or on the mountain.

For this reason it has an immensely deep meaning that

the Gospel is entirely in accord with what we have just described, and that this is drawn from the occult understanding of the conditions of nature. The Gospel brings this out clearly and it is factually correct in an occult sense. Hence we shall always see the following. When it is said that something took place by the lake, when being by the lake is referred to, definite forces are being applied and healing powers or powers of vision are unfolded. Thus Christ Jesus appears to His disciples by the lake in imagination only since He Himself is involved in the entire episode because of His capacity to exteriorize Himself. Although they do not have Him there in the physical body, the disciples see Him. In such an experience separation in space has no importance. He was together "with them" by the lake. For the same reason when reference is made to the soul forces of the apostles, the "mountain" is spoken of, as it was when the Twelve were appointed and their souls were enjoined to take into themselves the group soul of Elijah. And when the Christ wished to appear in the whole grandeur of His world-historical and cosmic manifestation, again the mountain is spoken of. The Transfiguration therefore takes place on the mountain.

It is indeed from this point of view that we must picture the scene of the Transfiguration. The three disciples Peter, James, and John prove themselves to be capable of being initiated into the deeper secrets of the Mystery of Golgotha. To the clairvoyant eyes of these three which were now opened there appeared, transfigured, that is in their spiritual nature, Elijah on the one side and Moses on the other, with Christ Jesus Himself in the middle. And it is imaginatively indicated in the Gospel that Christ was now in the form in which in His spiritual nature He could be recognized. This is shown with sufficient clarity in the Mark Gospel:

> And He was transfigured before them.
> And His garments became gleaming bright, brighter than any fuller on earth could bleach them.

148

And there appeared to them Elijah with Moses, and they
conversed with Jesus. (9: 2-4.)

After the great monologue of God comes a conversation
among these three. What a wonderful dramatic crescendo!
Everywhere the Gospels are full of such artistic sequences.
Indeed they are wonderfully composed. After hearing the
monologue of God we now have a conversation among these
three, and what a conversation! First we see Elijah and
Moses, one on each side of Christ Jesus. What is the significance of Elijah and Moses?

The figure of Moses has long been familiar to you; even
from the occult standpoint it has often been illuminated.
We know that world-historical wisdom chose to bridge the
span between primeval ages and the Mystery of Golgotha indirectly through Moses. We know from our studies on the
Luke Gospel that in the Jesus boy of whom Matthew especially speaks the reincarnated Zarathustra is to be seen. We
know also that this Zarathustra through all that belonged to
him and was in him made preparations for his later appearance on earth. I have often mentioned how through special
occult processes Zarathustra gave away his etheric body,
which then passed over into Moses so that Zarathustra's
etheric body was active in him. Thus when Elijah and
Moses are pictured next to Christ Jesus we have, so to
speak, in Moses those forces destined to lead over from
primitive forms of culture to what mankind was later to be
given in Christ Jesus and the Mystery of Golgotha.

But from another point of view we also have a transitional
figure in Moses. We know that he not only had within him
the etheric body of Zarathustra, which enabled him to bear
within himself the wisdom of Zarathustra which could then
become active in him, but we know also that Moses was in a
certain way initiated into the secrets of other peoples. In the
meeting with the Midianite priest Jethro we have to see a
special scene of initiation, as we have discussed before. This

149

is to be found in the Old Testament (Exodus 2: 16–21). Here it is clearly pointed out how Moses visits this lonely priest and not only learns from him the secrets of the initiation of Judaism but also those of other peoples. He bears all these within his inner being which has already experienced the special strengthening that came from the etheric body of Zarathustra. So there entered into the Jewish people through Moses the secrets of initiation of the whole surrounding world, thus enabling him to prepare, on a lower stage, as it were, what was to come about through Christ Jesus. This then was one of the streams that was to lead to the Mystery of Golgotha.

The other stream, as I have also indicated before, derived from what by this time was living in a natural way in the Jewish people, as a people. Moses was the individuality who as far as was possible in his time allowed the other stream that was in the world to pour into that stream that flowed through the generations from Abraham, Isaac and Jacob. But at the same time we should always keep in mind what was especially connected with the nature of the Hebrew people. Why had this people been chosen? Their task was to prepare for that era that we tried to call before our souls when, for example, we referred to Hellenism, and then when yesterday we spoke of Empedocles. We were referring in this way to that time when the ancient clairvoyant capacities were disappearing from men, when they lost their ability to see into the spiritual world, when the power of judgment took its place; and judgment is the special characteristic of the ego, when the ego emerges as an independent entity.

It was for the purpose of bringing to the ego all that could be given to the natural being of man through the organization of the blood that the Hebrew people were chosen. Absolutely everything that can be fully experienced through the physical organization of the human being had

150

to be experienced fully by this people. Man's intellectuality is certainly bound to his physical organization; and from the physical organization of the ancient Hebrew people was to be taken that which truly could nourish those human capacities that are dependent on the intellect. By contrast other peoples had to allow what comes from without, from initiation, to shine into their earthly organization, whereas what was able to rise up in man's own being through the blood relationship was to rise up through this relationship in the ancient Hebrew people. For this reason it was insisted on that this blood connection be a continuous one, and that every Hebrew carried within himself those capacities that have been flowing through the blood since the time of Abraham, Isaac and Jacob. The ego, bound to the blood, had to be conveyed to the physical organization through the blood of the ancient Hebrew people, and this could come about only through the medium of heredity.

I have already pointed out that the Old Testament story of the sacrifice of Isaac by Abraham and the manner in which it was prevented indicates how this people was specially chosen by the Godhead to be a gift to humanity, so that the outer physical vessel for egohood could be given to mankind. That this physical vessel, the ancient Jewish people, was a gift of God to humanity is indicated by Abraham's willingness to sacrifice his son. If he had sacrificed Isaac, Abraham would at the same time have sacrificed that physical organization that was to give mankind the physical basis for the intellect, and thus for egohood. In receiving back his son Abraham received back the whole God-given organization. This is the great significance of the restoration of Isaac (Genesis 22: 1-19). At the same time it is also indicated that on the one side there is the spiritual stream pictured for us in the Transfiguration scene in the person of Moses, and this is now to flow onward precisely through the instrument of the Jewish people as far as the deed of the

Mystery of Golgotha. What then is pictured for us in the person of Elijah?

Through him the totality of the divine revelation living in the Jewish people unites with what happens through the Mystery of Golgotha. In the book of *Numbers* it is shown in the 25th chapter how Israel is led astray into idolatry, but is rescued through the agency of one man. Through the decisiveness of one man the Israelites, the ancient Hebrew people, were not totally given over to idolatry at that time. Who is this man? It is he of whom we are told in the book of *Numbers* that he had the strength to come before the ancient Hebrew people who were in danger of lapsing into the idolatry of the surrounding peoples, and to intercede with the God who had been revealed through Moses. This was truly a strong soul. This intercession with God is usually translated into the German language as "eifern," and in English as "be zealous." This zeal is not to be thought of in any bad sense; it simply means to intercede strongly. Thus we read in *Numbers* 25: 10–12:

> And the Lord spoke with Moses and said: "Phinehas, the son of Eleazar, the son of Aaron the priest, has turned away my anger from the children of Israel through his zeal concerning me. So in my zeal I have not destroyed the children of Israel. Therefore say: See, I give him my covenant of peace."

Yahweh said this to Moses. And in this particular passage we must also see something that according to ancient Hebrew esoteric teaching is exceptionally significant. This is confirmed by occult research. We know that those representing the high priesthood of ancient Israel are direct descendants of Aaron, and that in them the essence of what was given to mankind by the Jewish people lives on. At that moment of world history, according to Hebrew esoteric teaching and confirmed by more recent occult research, the significant truth was indicated that Yahweh imparts the knowledge to Moses that in Phinehas, the son of Eleazar, the grandson of Aaron, he was bestowing on the Hebrew people a very special priest who represents him and is closely connected with him. And the esoteric teaching and occult research reveal that the same soul lives in the body of Phinehas that was later present in Elijah. Thus we have a continuous line of descent which in several points we have already described. In Aaron's grandson we have one soul that is of concern to us, the soul that lives in Phinehas. The same soul appears again in Elijah-Naboth and then in John the Baptist, and we know how it continues throughout the evolution of mankind. So there is pictured for us this soul on the one side of the Christ, and on the other the soul of Moses himself.

So in the Transfiguration, in the Transformation on the mountain, we have before us a streaming together of the entire spirituality of earth evolution, the essence of which flowed through the Jewish blood into the Levitical line. Thus the soul of Phinehas, the son of Eleazar, the son of Aaron stands before us; Moses stands before us; and there stands before us also He who fulfilled the Mystery of Golgotha. And the three disciples who were to be initiated, Peter, James and John, were to perceive in imaginative knowledge how these forces, these spiritual streams, flowed together. When yesterday I tried to picture for you how something like a call sounds over from Greece to Palestine and the call that answered it, this was something more than a mere pictorial description of the facts. It was indeed a preparation for that great world-historical discourse that now actually took place. The disciples Peter, James, and John were to be initiated into what these three souls had to discuss together; one soul who belonged to the people of the Old Testament, one who carried within himself much of what we know about the Moses soul, while the third, as cosmic deity, is uniting Himself with the earth. This the disciples were to see.

We know that it could not immediately enter into their hearts, nor could they understand immediately what was revealed to them. But this is customary with much that is experienced in the realm of the occult. It is experienced imaginatively. One does not understand it, and often learns to understand it only in the following incarnation. But then our understanding is better able to adapt itself to what had previously been seen. We can *feel* how on the mountain there were the three cosmic powers, while down below were the three who were to be initiated into these great cosmic secrets. And from all these things the feeling can arise in our souls that the Gospel, if we understand it correctly, and especially if we allow the dramatic intensification and the artistic composition which is itself an expression everywhere of cosmic facts, does truly point to the great revolution that really happened at the time of the Mystery of Golgotha.

When the Gospel is explained through occult research it speaks a very clear language indeed. In the future it will become important that people should recognize ever more clearly what is the issue at stake, and what is particularly significant in one or the other passage in the Gospel; and only then will we be able to grasp the point that is of special importance in a particular parable, or in one story or another. It is strange how ordinary theologians or philosophers when they try to explain the most important things in the Gospels actually always take their point of departure as if they were not putting the horse before the cart in the usual way but the other way round—or, as we say in common parlance, they "put the cart before the horse." This indeed happens with so many interpreters and commentators; they miss the main point.

We wish to draw your attention now to a passage that you will find in the fourteenth chapter of the Mark Gospel.

We do this because it is of great significance for the progress of our studies.

> And while he was at Bethany in the house of Simon the leper, a woman came in as he sat at table with an alabaster flask of genuine costly ointment of nard, and she broke the flask open and poured the ointment over his head.
>
> But some of those present disputed among themselves and said, "Why this waste of ointment?" It could have been sold for more than three hundred denarii that could have been given to the poor. And they were indignant with her.
>
> But Jesus said, "Let her alone, why do you trouble her? She has accomplished a good work in me. For you have the poor with you all the time and you can do good to them whenever you wish. But you do not have me with you forever. She has done what she could; she has anointed my body in advance for burial.
>
> I say truly to you, wherever in the whole world this Gospel is proclaimed, her deed will be spoken of in her memory." (Mark 14: 3-9.)

It would surely be a good thing if we were to admit that this passage contains something striking in it. Most people, if they are honest, ought to confess that they are forced to sympathize with those who complained that the ointment was wasted, and that in any event it was unnecessary to pour it over someone's head. Most people will indeed believe it would have been better to sell the ointment for three hundred denarii and give the money to the poor. And if you are honest perhaps you will find that Christ was being callous when He said that it was better to let her do what she wished to do instead of giving the three hundred denarii to the poor, a sum that the ointment would have realized if it had been sold. At this point, if we are not to be shocked by the whole story, we must say to ourselves that there must be something else behind this. Indeed, the Gospel goes further, and in this passage it is not at all polite. For it seems to

155

imply that if you can find a number of people who admit that it would have been better to give to the poor the three hundred denarii that could have been obtained for the ointment, then these people are thinking like a certain other person. For it continues:

> "Wherever in the whole world this Gospel is proclaimed, her deed will also be spoken of in her memory."
> And Judas Iscariot, one of the Twelve, went to the chief Priests to deliver him up to them. And they were glad when they heard it, and promised to give him money. And he sought how he could find a good opportunity to deliver him up. (14: 9–12.)

That is to say, because Judas Iscariot was specially offended by the spilling of the ointment—and the others who took offense at the spilling of the ointment are thereby associated with the example of Judas—so the Gospel is by no means even polite, for it points out with the utmost clarity that those who took offense at the spilling of the ointment are exactly like Judas Iscariot, who later sold the Lord for thirty silver pieces. What the Gospel is saying is that Judas is too fond of money, and so are the people who wish to sell the ointment for three hundred denarii. We should never gloss over the Gospel, for glossing over such passages prevents an objective, correct interpretation. What we must do is find out what is the real issue. And we shall find many more examples to show us how the Gospel sometimes even persists in giving incidental details in a rather offensive manner if the purpose is to cast an especially clear light on a particular point.

What is the real question at issue in this passage? The Gospel wishes to tell us that it is man's task not to look only at sense existence, nor to suppose that only those things are important that have value and meaning in sense existence. Beyond everything else man should take the supersensible world into himself, and it is important to pay attention also to things that no longer have any meaning for sense existence. The body of Christ Jesus, which was anointed in advance by the woman before its burial, has no meaning if it is dead; but we should also do something for what has value and meaning beyond sense existence. This had to be especially strongly emphasized. For this reason something was made use of, to which even the natural human consciousness in the life of the senses attaches great value. The Gospel here chooses a special example to show how sometimes something must be withdrawn from sense life and offered to the spirit, to the ego after its liberation from the body. Just at this moment the Gospel chooses what is apparently an irreverent example; something is taken away from the poor that is given to the spirit, given to the ego when it has been freed from the body. It does not look at what gives value to earth existence but at what can come into the ego and can radiate forth from it. This is pictured here in a very powerful manner, by bringing it into relation with Judas Iscariot, who commits a treacherous deed because he feels himself at heart especially impelled toward sense existence, and associates with those who are described in far from courteous terms as the real Philistines, not too strong a word for those who are clearly indicated in this passage. Judas is concerned only with what has meaning in sense existence, in the same way as those who believe that what can be bought for three hundred denarii has more importance than that which transcends the life of sense.

Everywhere in the Gospels attention is directed to the main point and not to side issues; and the Gospel will be recognized wherever the spiritual is recognized. This example will be recognized as pertinent wherever the spiritual is truly recognized. Wherever one wishes to exalt the value of the supersensible for the ego, it will always be said that the wasting of the ointment was a matter of no importance.

There is another remarkable passage where it is again possible to perceive the methodically artistic manner in which the Gospel veils the occult facts concerned with the evolution of mankind. This passage is again a difficult puzzle for the commentators.

> And the next day, as they were leaving Bethany he was hungry.
> And from afar he saw a fig tree, which had leaves. So he went to see if he might find something on it. And when he came to it he found nothing but leaves, for it was not the season for figs.
> And he began to speak to it, "Never to all eternity shall anyone eat fruit from you!" And his disciples heard it. (Mark 11: 12-14.)

Now we should all ask ourselves honestly, "Is it not truly extraordinary that, according to the Gospel, a God should go straight up to a fig tree, look for figs and find none, and then the reason is explicitly given why He did not find any—it was not the time for figs—so at a time when there are no figs He goes up to the fig tree, looks for figs and finding none, says, "Never to all eternity shall anyone eat fruit from you?"

Now consider the usual explanations given of this story —although the Gospel gives nothing but the dry and prosaic fact that for some strange reason Christ Jesus feels hunger, and goes up to a fig tree at a time when no figs grow. He finds no figs, and then curses the tree telling it that to all eternity no figs will grow any more on it. What, then is the fig tree, and why is the entire story told here? Anyone who can read occult works first of all will recognize in the fig tree (its connection with the Gospel will be shown later) the same picture as was spoken of in relation to the Buddha, who sat under the Bodhi tree and received enlightenment for his sermon at Benares. "Under the Bodhi tree" means the same as "under the fig tree." From a world-historical point of view it was still the "time of figs" in respect to human clairvoyance, that is to say it was possible to receive enlightenment as the Buddha did, under the Bodhi tree, under the fig tree. But this was no longer true, and that is what the disciples had to learn. From the point of view of world history it was a fact that there was no longer any fruit on the tree under which the Buddha had received his enlightenment.

And what was happening in all of mankind was mirrored at that time in the soul of Christ. We may see in Empedocles of Sicily a representative of humanity, a representative of many people who were similarly hungry because their souls could no longer discover the revelation that had been given earlier and had to be satisfied with the abstractions of the ego. In the same way that we can speak of the starving Empedocles, we can speak of the hunger for the spirit that all men felt in the times that were then beginning. And the entire hunger of mankind discharged itself into the soul of Christ Jesus as the Mystery of Golgotha approached. The disciples were to participate in this secret and know of it.

Christ led them to the fig tree and told them the secret of the Bodhi tree, omitting to tell them, because it had no significance for them, that the Buddha was still able to find fruit on it. Now it was no longer the "time of figs," figs that the Buddha had received from the Bodhi tree when he gave his sermon at Benares. Now Christ had to tell them that for all eternity the fruit of knowledge would never again ripen on the tree from which the light of Benares had shown down, but that hereafter the light would shine from the Mystery of Golgotha.

What is the truth that is presented to us here? The truth that Christ Jesus went with His disciples from Bethany to Jerusalem, and that a specially strong feeling, a specially strong force was called forth in the disciples, awakening clairvoyant forces in their souls, so that they were predisposed toward imagination. Clairvoyant imaginative powers

159

were awakened in the disciples. In clairvoyance they see the Bodhi tree, the fig tree, and Christ Jesus inspires in them the knowledge that the fruit of knowledge can no longer come from the Bodhi tree, for it is no longer the "time of figs," that is of the ancient knowledge. For all eternity the tree will be withered, but a new tree must grow forth, a tree consisting of the dead wood of the cross; a tree on which the fruit of ancient knowledge will not ripen, but the fruit that can ripen for mankind from the Mystery of Golgotha, which is linked as by a new symbol to the cross on Golgotha. In the place of that scene of world history when the Buddha sat under the Bodhi tree stands the picture of Golgotha where another tree, the tree of the cross, is raised, on which hung the living fruit of the God-man revealing himself, so that from Him may radiate the new knowledge of the fruit of the ever growing tree that will bear fruit to all eternity.

LECTURE 9

It has been repeatedly pointed out in the course of these lectures how, as time goes on, the relationship of mankind to the Gospels will be fundamentally changed through the recognition of their profoundly artistic character, and the artistry of their composition. The occult background and the world-historical impulses pictured in the Gospels will be seen in the right light only when their artistic composition is taken into account. During the entire course of the historical evolution of mankind, the art and literature of the Gospels are linked together in the same way, as we have been able to point out on a few occasions in the course of these lectures.

We have pointed to those lonely figures in the Hellenic world who experienced in their souls the gradual disappearance and dying out of the old clairvoyant vision, for which they had to exchange the consciousness of the present time, its abstract concepts and abstract ideas, out of which the ego of man has to work. We can also point to something else which, precisely in Greek culture, from a certain point of view represents a kind of concluding phase of the culture of mankind. It is as if this culture had attained a certain peak, and had to be enkindled again from another point of view. I am referring to Greek art. How did it happen that people at the time of the Renaissance in Europe sought in their souls the land of the Greeks, that is to say the land of Beauty, and saw an ideal of human development in the wonderful way in which the Greeks shaped the human form? But this did not only occur in the time of the Renaissance. In the modern classical epoch spirits like Goethe sought in the same way within their souls this land of the Greeks, the land of beautiful form. The reason for this is that in actual fact it was in Greece that beauty, which speaks out of external form directly to human sight, came to a kind of end, an end that indeed represented a certain high point of achievement.

In Greek beauty and Greek art everything confronts us enclosed in form. The composition of Greek works of art reveals to our sight exactly what is intended by the composition. It is there in sense existence, fully apparent to the eye. The greatness of Greek art consists in the fact that it has come forth so fully into outward appearance. We may say that the art of the Gospels also represents a new beginning, but one that to this day has scarcely been understood at all. There is above all in the Gospels an inner composition and an inner interweaving of artistic threads, which are also at the same time occult threads. As we emphasized yesterday the important thing is everywhere to look for the real point, as it is drawn to our attention in every description and every story.

It is particularly shown in the Mark Gospel, not so much in the wording but in the general tone of the presentation, that Christ is to be seen as a cosmic being, an earthly and supra-earthly manifestation, while the Mystery of Golgotha is shown as an earthly and supra-earthly fact. But something else is also emphasized, and here we are faced with the fine artistic element, especially toward the end of the Gospel. It is emphasized that a cosmic element is shining into the concerns of earth. It truly shines in; and it was the task of earth beings, of earthly human beings to bring their understanding to this impulse. Perhaps nowhere else is it indicated so well as in the Mark Gospel how fundamentally the whole of earth evolution will be necessary to enable us to understand what shone here out of the cosmos into earth existence, and how at the time of the Mystery of Golgotha such understanding was altogether impossible. And even today this

162

understanding is still absent. The truth that at that time there was only an initial impetus toward an understanding that can come into being only with the further development of mankind is shown in a quite wonderful way in the artistic composition of the Gospel. We can discern something of this artistic composition if we enquire into the form of understanding that could have been possible and brought to bear on the Mystery of Golgotha at the time it took place.

Essentially three kinds of understanding were possible, and they could arise at three different levels. Firstly, understanding could have been found in those who were nearest to Christ Jesus, His chosen disciples. They are presented to us everywhere in the Gospels as those whom the Lord Himself had chosen, to whom He confided many things to help them toward a higher understanding of existence. From them, therefore, we have a right to expect the greatest understanding of the Mystery of Golgotha. What kind of understanding may we expect from them? As we approach the end of the Mark Gospel this is ever more delicately interwoven into its composition. It is pointed out to us very clearly that these chosen disciples could have had a higher understanding than the leaders of the Old Testament people. But we must everywhere look for the point to which we are referring.

In Mark chapter 12, verses 18 to 27 you will find a conversation between Christ Jesus and the Sadducees, a conversation that is primarily concerned with the immortality of the soul. If the Gospels are read superficially it will not occur to anybody to ask why this conversation appears precisely here, a conversation about immortality followed by the curious question posed by the Sadducees, who spoke as follows, "It could happen that one of seven brothers married a woman but he dies, and the same woman marries the second. After the death of the second she also marries the third, and likewise with the others. She herself dies only after the death of the seventh brother." The Sadducees could not understand how, if there is indeed immortality, these seven men should behave toward the one woman in the spiritual world. This is a well-known Sadducean objection which, as some of you may know, was not made only at the time of the Mystery of Golgotha but is even to be found in some modern books as an objection to immortality, which proves that in the circles where such books are written there is still no complete understanding of the matter. But why was this conversation recorded? If we consider the matter, we shall see that the answer given by Christ Jesus tells us clearly that souls become heavenly after death, that there is no marrying among beings of the supra-earthly world. In the case cited by the Sadducees the facts are totally irrelevant, since they are concerned with a relationship that is essentially earthly and has no meaning beyond the earth. In other words Christ Jesus is here speaking of circumstances prevailing in the extraterrestrial worlds which He wishes to bring in here solely for the contribution they can make to the understanding of life beyond the earth.

But as you approach the end of the Mark Gospel you will find still another conversation when Christ Jesus is asked about marriage (10: 1-12). This was a conversation between Christ Jesus and the Jewish scribes. How is it possible, He was asked, to dismiss a wife with a letter of divorce as permitted by the law of Moses? What was the reason for the answer given by Christ Jesus, "Yes, Moses gave you this law because your hearts are hard and you need an arrangement like this?" The reason is that He is now speaking about something entirely different. He is now speaking about how men and women were together before human evolution had been exposed to temptation through the Luciferic powers. That is to say, He is talking about something cosmic, something supra-earthly; He raised the subject to the supra-earthly plane. The reason for His answer is that He was leading the conversation beyond what refers simply to earthly life, beyond experience of the senses, beyond ordinary earth evolution. And this is already a significant example of how by appearing on earth He brings down to it supra-earthly, cosmic matters, and talks about such cosmic matters with the beings of earth.

By whom might we hope, or even go as far as to demand, that such discourses of Christ concerning these cosmic matters will be best understood? By those whom He had first chosen as His disciples. So the first form of understanding could be characterized in this way. The chosen disciples of Christ Jesus could have understood the Mystery of Golgotha in such a way that they could have interpreted the supra-earthly, cosmic aspect of this world-historical fact. This might have been expected from those disciples whom He had chosen.

A second kind of understanding could have been expected to be found among the leaders of the ancient Hebrew people, from the high priests, the chief justices, from those who knew the Scriptures and knew the historical evolution of the Old Testament people. What could have been asked of them? The Gospel shows clearly that they were not called upon to understand the realities of Christ Jesus, but they were expected to understand the fact that Christ Jesus came to the ancient Hebrew people, that with His individuality He was born into the blood of the people, that He was a Son of the House of David, inwardly linked to the essence of what came through David into the Jewish people. This is the second and lesser kind of understanding. That Christ Jesus had a mission that marked the high point of the mission of the whole Jewish people is indicated in a wonderful way toward the end of the Mark Gospel when it is shown ever more clearly—see in what a delicately artistic way this is indicated—that here we have to do with the Son of David. Thus, while the disciples were called upon to have an understanding of the mission of the cosmic hero, those who considered themselves as belonging to the Jewish people were called upon to understand the truth that the time had come for the completion of the mission of David. That is the second kind of understanding. The Jewish people should have known that the end of their old mission had come and that there could come a new flaming up of their own particular mission.

And the third kind of comprehension—where should this have been found? Again something lesser is demanded, and it is remarkable with what delicacy the artistic composition of the Mark Gospel indicates it. Something lesser is demanded and this lesser element was required of the Romans. Read what happens toward the end of this Gospel when Christ Jesus is delivered over to the Romans by the high priests—I am referring only to this Mark Gospel. The high priests ask Christ Jesus if He wishes to speak of the Christ and acknowledge Himself as the Christ, at which they would take offense, because He would then be speaking of His cosmic mission; or if He wishes to speak of the fact that He is a scion of the House of David. But why does Pilate, the Roman, take offense? Simply because Christ was supposed to have claimed He was the "king of the Jews" (15: 1-15). The Jews were expected to understand that He represented the culminating point in their own development. The Romans were expected to understand that He signified something in the development of the Jewish people —not a climax of this development but something that was to play a leading part in it. If the Romans had understood this what would have been the result? Nothing much different from what came about in any case; only they failed to understand it. We know that Judaism spread indirectly over the whole Western world by way of Alexandria. The Romans could have had some understanding for the fact that the moment in world history had arrived for the spread of Jewish culture. Such an understanding was again less than what the scribes ought to have understood. The Romans were called upon to understand simply the significance of the Jews as a part of the world. That they did not understand this, which would have been a task of that age, is shown through the fact that Pilate did not understand why Christ Jesus was looked upon as the king of the Jews, and regarded it, indeed, as a harmless matter that He should have been presented as a king of the Jews.

Thus a threefold understanding of the mission of Christ Jesus might have been expected: first, that the chosen disciples could have had an understanding of Christ as a cosmic being, secondly, the understanding that the Jews were supposed to have for what was burgeoning in the Jewish people itself, and thirdly the understanding that the Romans ought to have had of the Jewish people, how they were ceasing to expand only over Palestine, but were beginning to spread over the greater part of the earth.

This secret is concealed in the artistic composition especially of the Mark Gospel; and in it answers are given, and with great clarity, to all three questions.

The first question must be: Are the apostles, the chosen disciples equal to the task of comprehension imposed on them? Did they recognize Christ as a cosmic spirit? Did they recognize that there in their midst was one who was not only what He signified to them as man, but who was enveloped in an aura through which cosmic forces and cosmic laws were transmitted to the earth? Did they understand this?

That Christ Jesus demanded such an understanding from them is clearly indicated in the Gospel. For when the two disciples, the sons of Zebedee, came to Him and asked that one of them might sit on His right hand and the other on His left, He said to them, "You do not know what you ask. Can you drink from the cup that I drink, or be baptized with the baptism with which I am baptized?" (10: 38.)

It is clearly indicated here that Christ Jesus required this of them, and at first they solemnly pledge themselves to it. What might then have happened? There were two possibilities. One would have been that the chosen disciples would really have passed in company with Christ through all that is known as the Mystery of Golgotha, and that the bond between Christ and the disciples would have been preserved until the Mystery of Golgotha. That was one of the two things that could have happened. But it is made very clear, especially in the Mark Gospel, that exactly the opposite occurred. When Christ Jesus was taken prisoner, everyone fled, and Peter who had promised solemnly that he would take offense at nothing, denied him three times before the cock crowed twice. That is the picture presented from the point of view of the apostles. But how is it shown that, from the point of view of the Christ, it was not at all like this?

Let us place ourselves with all humility—as we must— within the soul of Christ Jesus, who to the end tries to maintain the woven bond linking Him with the souls of the disciples. Let us place ourselves as far as we may within the soul of Christ Jesus during the events that followed. This soul might well put to itself the world-historical question, "Is it possible for me to cause the souls of at least the most select of the disciples to rise to the height of experiencing with me everything that is to happen until the Mystery of Golgotha?" The soul of Christ itself is faced with this question at the crucial moment when Peter, James and John are led out to the Mount of Olives, and Christ Jesus wants to find out from within Himself whether He will be able to keep those whom He had chosen. On the way He becomes anguished. Yes, my friends, does anyone believe, can anyone believe that Christ became anguished in face of death, of the Mystery of Golgotha, and that He sweated blood because of

168

the approaching event of Golgotha? Anyone who could believe that would show he had little understanding for the Mystery of Golgotha; it may be in accord with theology, but it shows no insight. Why does the Christ become distressed? He does not tremble before the cross. That goes without saying. He is distressed above all in face of this question, "Will those whom I have with me here stand the test of this moment when it will be decided whether they want to accompany me in their souls, whether they want to experience everything with me until the cross?" It had to be decided if their consciousness could remain sufficiently awake so that they could experience everything with Him until the cross. This was the "cup" that was coming near to Him. So He leaves them alone to see if they can stay "awake," that is in a state of consciousness in which they can experience with Him what He is to experience. Then He goes aside and prays, "Father, let this cup pass from me, but let it be done according to your will, not mine." In other words, "Let it not be my experience to stand quite alone as the Son of Man, but may the others be permitted to go with me."

He comes back, and they are asleep; they could not maintain their state of wakeful consciousness. Again He makes the attempt, and again they could not maintain it. So it becomes clear to Him that He is to stand alone, and that they will not participate in the path to the cross. The cup had not passed away from Him. He was destined to accomplish the deed in loneliness, a loneliness that was also of the soul. Certainly the world had the Mystery of Golgotha, but at the time it happened it had as yet no understanding of this event; and the most select and chosen disciples could not stay awake to that point. This therefore is the first kind of understanding; and it comes to expression with the most consummate artistry if we can only understand how to feel the actual occult background that lies concealed behind the words of the Gospels.

Let us now enquire into the second kind of understand-

169

ing, and ask how the Jewish leaders understood the one who was to come forth from the lineage of David as the flower of the old Hebrew development. We find in the tenth chapter of the Mark Gospel one of the first passages in which it is pointed out to us what understanding the ancient Hebrew people showed toward the one who arose from the lineage of David. This is the decisive passage when Christ Jesus is approaching Jerusalem, and should have been recognized by the old Hebrew people as the successor of David.

> And they came to Jericho. And as he was leaving Jericho with his disciples and a considerable crowd, a blind man, Bartimaeus, the son of Timaeus, was sitting by the road, begging. And when he heard that it was Jesus of Nazareth, he began to call, "Jesus, thou Son of David, have mercy on me." And many scolded him, telling him to be silent. But he called all the more loudly, "Thou Son of David, have mercy on me." (10: 46–48.)

It is explicitly stated that the call of the blind man was expressed in the words "Thou Son of David," showing that he could reach the understanding only of "the Son of David."

And Jesus stood still and said, "Call him here." And they called the blind man and said to him, "Be of good cheer, arise, he is calling you."

So he threw off his mantle, jumped up and came to Jesus.

And Jesus said to him, "What do you want me to do for you?"

The blind man said to him, "Rabboni, that I may receive my sight."

And Jesus said to him. "Cheer up!* Your faith has res-

---

*Although this is not the meaning usually given in the biblical translations, the Greek word used here (hypage) ordinarily has the meaning given here and I prefer it to the not particularly meaningful "Go" or "Go thy way" or "go along" customarily used. Ed.

cued you." And immediately he received his sight and followed him on his way.

It was therefore only faith that was required of him. Is it not worthwhile giving consideration to why, among the other stories, the healing of a blind man is referred to? Why does the story stand there all by itself? We should learn something from the way the Gospel is composed. It is not the cure itself that is at issue, but that only one man among them all, and he a blind man, should call with all his strength, "Jesus, thou Son of David!" Those who had sight did not recognize Him, but the blind man, who does not see Him physically at all, does recognize Him. So what has to be shown here is how blind the others are, and that this man had to be blind in order to see Him. In this passage what is important is the blindness, not the healing; and it shows at the same time how little Christ was understood.

As we proceed further we find how He speaks everywhere of how the cosmic lives in the individual human being. Indeed, He speaks of the cosmic when He speaks of immortality, and it is noteworthy how He speaks of this just in connection with His appearance as the Son of David. He proclaims that God is a God of the living and not of the dead, the God of Abraham, Isaac and Jacob (12: 26-27), because Abraham, Isaac and Jacob live on in their successors in different forms, in that God lives in their individualities. This is pointed out still more strongly when Christ refers to what slumbers within man and must be awakened. Here it is said that it was not a question of a merely physical son of David, for David himself speaks of the "Lord" and not of a physical son (12: 35-37). As the influence of the cosmic Christ is waning, everywhere reference is made to the "Lord" that lives within the individuality of man, and how this is to spring from the lineage of David.

We wish to draw attention to one particular passage that

you will find near the end of the Mark Gospel. It is a passage
that can easily be overlooked if it is not understood, though
it is indeed a soul-shattering passage. It occurs where it is
reported that Christ has now been delivered over to the
worldly powers, that He is to be condemned, and excuses
are sought for condeming Him. Just before this passage
what He did in the Temple was described, how He drove
out the money-changers and overturned their tables, and
how He preached most remarkable words which were heard
in the souls of those present. Yet nothing happened to Him
because of this. Christ explicitly draws attention to this
when He says, "You have heard all this. Yet now, when I
am standing before you, you are looking for false charges
against me. You have taken me prisoner by the customary
method of employing a traitor, as if you were arresting
someone who has committed a serious crime whereas you
did nothing while I stood among you in the Temple."

This is indeed a shattering passage, for we are given to
understand that essentially, wherever Christ is active,
nothing can be done against Him. Is it not permissible to
ask why? Indeed, He is working so actively that He points
with the utmost clarity to the fact that a turning point in
cosmic evolution has been reached, as He indicates with the
words, "The first shall be last and the last shall be first."
(9: 35.) Such teachings that He hurls at them must have
seemed terrifying by comparison with the teachings of the
Old Testament and the way they understood them. Yet
nothing happens. Afterwards He is captured under cover of
darkness and night by the agency of a traitor; and we even
have the impression that there was something like a struggle
when He was captured. The passage is truly shattering:

But the traitor had given them a sign and said, "The one
whom I will kiss, it is he; seize and secure him."
And when he came he went directly to Him and said

"Rabbi, Rabbi!" and kissed him. And they laid hands on Him and seized Him.

But one of those who were standing by drew his sword and struck at a servant of the high priest and cut off his ear.

And Jesus spoke to them, "You have come out with swords and sticks to take me prisoner as you would a murderer. I was daily in the Temple teaching, and you did not seize me; but the Scriptures must be fulfilled." (14: 44–49.)

What was it that really happened that they did not at first capture Him, and then sought reasons to capture Him like a murderer? It is only possible to understand what happened if we look at it in the light of occult truths. I have already pointed out how the Mark Gospel clearly describes occult and spiritual facts intermingled at random with purely physical facts. And we shall show how Christ clearly does not limit His activity to the deeds of the single personality, Jesus of Nazareth. He worked upon His disciples when He came to them by the lake in an external form but outside His physical body. So while His physical body might be in one place or another, He could while outside it inspire into the souls of His disciples all that He did, and all that radiated from Him as spiritual impulse. And we shall point out that the Mark Gospel makes it abundantly clear how human beings hear what He preaches and teaches while He appears to them in an external form outside His physical body. What He says lives in their souls; though they do not understand it, it comes to life within their souls. In the individuality of Christ and in the crowd it is both earthly and supra-earthly at the same time.

The Christ is everywhere connected with a widely extended, actively working aura. This aura was present and active because He was linked with the souls of those whom He had chosen, and it remained present as long as He was linked to them. The cup had not passed away from Him; the chosen human beings had shown no comprehension. So this aura gradually withdrew from the man Jesus of Nazareth; Christ became ever more estranged from the Son of Man, Jesus of Nazareth. Toward the end of His life Jesus of Nazareth was more and more alone, and the Christ became ever more loosely connected with Him.

Although the cosmic element was there until the moment pictured as that of the sweating of blood in Gethsemane, and Christ up to this moment was fully united with Jesus of Nazareth, now through the failure of human beings to understand this connection the link was loosened. And whereas earlier the cosmic Christ was active in the temple and drove out the money-changers, expounding mighty teachings, and nothing happened to Him, now, when Jesus of Nazareth was only loosely connected with the Christ the posse could come near Him. However, we can still see the cosmic element present, but less and less connected with the Son of Man. This is what makes the whole episode so soul-shattering! Because the threefold understanding could not be forthcoming, what did the men finally have in their hands? What could they seize, what could they condemn, what could they nail to the cross? The Son of Man! And the more they did all this, the more did the cosmic element withdraw that had entered the life of earth as a youthful impulse. It escaped them. For those who sentenced Him and carried out the judgment there remained only the Son of Man, around whom only hovered what was to come down to earth as a youthful cosmic element.

No Gospel other than that of St. Mark tells how only the Son of Man remained, and that the cosmic element only hovered around Him. Thus in no other Gospel do we perceive the cosmic fact in relation to the Christ event expressed with such clarity, the fact that at the very moment when men who failed to understand laid their violent human hands upon the Son of Man, the cosmic element escaped them. The youthful cosmic element which from that turn-

174

ing point of time entered earth evolution as an impulse, escaped. All that was left was the Son of Man; and this is clearly emphasized in the Mark Gospel. Let us read the passage and find out if the Mark Gospel does indeed emphasize how, just at this moment in the unfolding of events, the cosmic acts in relation to the human.

> And Jesus spoke to them, "You have set out with swords and sticks to take me prisoner, as if I were a murderer. I was daily with you in the temple teaching, and you did not seize me. But the Scriptures must be fulfilled."
> And they all forsook him and fled. (14: 48-50.)

He stands alone. But what has become of the youthful, cosmic element? Think of the loneliness of this man, permeated as He was by the cosmic Christ, who now confronts the posse like a murderer. And those who should have understood Him flee! "And they all forsook Him and fled," it says in the 50th verse. Then in verses 51 and 52:

> And there was a youth among his followers,* who wore a fine linen garment over his bare body, and they seized him. But he let go of the linen garment and fled naked.

Who is this youth? Who was it who escaped here? Who is it who appears here, next to Christ Jesus, nearly unclothed, and then slips away unclothed? This is the youthful cosmic impulse, it is the Christ who slips away, who now has only a loose connection with the Son of Man. Much is contained in these 51st and 52nd verses. The new impulse retains nothing of what former times were able to wrap around man. It is the entirely naked, new cosmic impulse of earth evolution. It remains with Jesus of Nazareth, and we find it again at the beginning of the sixteenth chapter.

---

*The Greek says "who was following him closely." Ed.

And when the Sabbath was over Mary Magdalene and
Mary the mother of James and Salome bought spices and
went there to anoint him. And early in the morning on the
first day of the week they came to the tomb as the sun was
rising.

And they said among themselves, "Who will roll away
the stone from the door of the tomb for us?" And when they
looked up they saw that the stone was rolled away, for it was
really very large.

And as they entered the tomb they saw a youth sitting on
the right side, clothed in a long white robe; and they were
startled.

But he said to them, "Do not be frightened. You seek
Jesus of Nazareth, the crucified one. He has risen!" (16: 1-6.)

This is the same youth. In the whole artistic composition
of the Gospels nowhere else does this youth confront us, the
youth who slips away from the people at the moment when
they condemn the Son of Man, who is there again when the
three days are over, and who from now onward is active as
the cosmic principle of the earth. Nowhere else in the Gospels—you should compare the others—except in these two
passages does this youth confront us, and in such a grandiose manner. Here we have all we need in order to understand the profound meaning of just this Gospel of St. Mark,
which is telling us that we have to do with a cosmic event,
with a cosmic Christ. Only now do we understand why the
remainder of the Mark Gospel had to be artistically composed as it was.

It is indeed remarkable that, after this significant appearance of the youth has come twice before us, the Gospel
quickly comes to an end, and all that remains are a few striking sentences. For it is scarcely possible to imagine that
anything that came later could have still yielded any further
enhancement. Perhaps the sublime and marvelous element
could have been enhanced, but not what is soul-shattering

and of significance for earth evolution. Consider again this composition of the Mark Gospel: the monologue of God; the cosmic conversation on the mountain above the earth to which the three disciples were called but did not understand; then Gethsemane, the scene on the Mount of Olives when Christ had to acknowledge that those who had been chosen could not attain to an understanding of what was about to happen; how He had to tread this path alone, how the Son of Man would suffer and be crucified. Then the world-historical loneliness of the Son of Man who is abandoned, abandoned by those He had chosen and then abandoned gradually by the cosmic principle. Thus, after we have understood the mission and significance of the youth who slips away from the eyes and hands of men, we come to understand in an especially profound manner the words, "My God, my God, why hast Thou forsaken me?" (15: 34.) Then the reappearance of the youth, whereupon it is briefly shown how the youth is a spiritual, supersensible being, who becomes sense-perceptible only through special circumstances, when He first shows himself to Mary Magdalene. Then afterward, "He revealed Himself in another form to two of them as they went for a walk into the countryside." (16: 12.) The physical could not have showed itself "in another form."

Then the Gospel quickly comes to an end, having indicated that what could not be understood at that time had to be left to the future. Humanity, which had then arrived at the deepest point of its descent, could only be directed toward the future, and it is in the way in which mankind is referred to the future that we can best appreciate the artistic composition of the Gospel. How may we suppose that such a reference to the future would emanate from one who had experienced this threefold failure to understand as He faced the fulfillment of the Mystery of Golgotha? We can imagine that He would point to the fact that the more we go forward into the future, the more men will have to gain an understanding of what happened at that time.

We shall only achieve the right understanding if we pay attention to what we can experience through the Mark Gospel which speaks to us in a remarkable way. If therefore we say to ourselves that every age has to bring more and more understanding to what happened at that time, and to what the Mystery of Golgotha really was—then we believe that with what we call here our anthroposophical movement we are in fact fulfilling for the first time something that is indicated here in this Gospel. We are bringing a new understanding to what the Christ wanted to come about in the world. This new comprehension is difficult. The possibility is always present that we may misunderstand the being of Christ; and this was already clearly indicated by Christ Himself:

> "And then if one says to you, 'See, here is Christ,' or, 'See, he is there,' don't believe it. For false Christs and false prophets will arise, and they will show signs and wonders to lead astray even the chosen ones if that should be possible.
> But you see to it! Behold, I have fortold everything to you." (13: 21-23.)

At all times since the event of Golgotha there has been ample opportunity to let such words be a warning to us. Whoever has ears to hear may also hear today how the word resounds over to us from Golgotha, "If someone says to you 'See, here is Christ,' or 'see, he is there,' don't believe it. For false Christs and false prophets will arise and show signs and wonders such as to lead astray if possible even the chosen ones."

How may we face up to the Mystery of Golgotha? Among the few striking sentences contained in the Mark Gospel after it has spoken to us in such a soul-shattering way is to be found also the very last sentence, in which it is related

178

how the disciples, who had earlier shown so little comprehension, after they had received a new impulse through
the youth, the cosmic Christ, "went forth and preached
everywhere, and the Lord worked with them, confirming
the word through the signs that accompanied it." (16: 20.)

The Lord worked with them! This we recognize as in accord with the meaning of the Mystery of Golgotha. Not that
"the Lord" could be incarnated anywhere in the physical
body, but where He is understood, if work is performed in
His name, then He works with us; and He is spiritually
among those who in truth understand His name—without
presenting Him, out of vanity, in a physical form. Rightly
understood the Gospel of St. Mark tells us about the Mystery of Golgotha itself in such a way that, when we rightly
understand it, we may also find the possibility of fulfilling
the Mystery of Golgotha in the right manner. Precisely in
what is contained only in this Mark Gospel, in this remarkable story of the youth who at a decisive moment broke
away, so to speak, from Christ Jesus, do we discover the in-
dication as to how this Gospel must be understood. Because
the chosen ones fled and they did not truly participate in
everything that happened afterward. This is also told in the
Gospel. In truly artistic fashion a passage is inserted in the
midst of the composition. A passage of the utmost clarity is
here inserted; yet none of the disciples were present, not
one of them was an eye-witness! And yet the whole story is
told! So the question is still presented to us, and we shall
try, in answering this question, to penetrate still further into
the matter, and at the same time to throw light upon the
remainder.

Where does this remainder originate that the disciples
have not seen? Jewish traditions relate the story quite differently from the way it appears here in the Gospels. Where
does it come from? What then is the real truth about the

Mystery of Golgotha since those who give an account of it were not themselves present? What is the source of their knowledge of something that none of those who have preached Christianity can have seen?

This question will lead us still more deeply into the matter.

LECTURE 10

We saw yesterday how a part of the life shared by Jesus and His chosen disciples is missing in the Mark Gospel, and indeed also in the others. Just those most closely connected with Him did not take any part in the events beginning with the period following His arrest, that is, the trial, condemnation and crucifixion of Christ Jesus. This again is a feature of the Gospel that is intentionally emphasized. To some extent the intention was to show how a path can be prepared to enable human beings to come to an understanding of the Mystery of Golgotha, how after the Mystery of Golgotha had been accomplished it would be possible to come to an understanding of the Mystery. For it is true that this understanding has to be acquired in a totally different way than is needed for the understanding of any other historical fact of human evolution. From what has happened just in our own times we can grasp this point most clearly.

Since the eighteenth century modern consciousness has been seeking, as we might say, a support for a belief in the Mystery of Golgotha; and this attempt has been made from various viewpoints and the search has gone through various phases. Until the eighteenth century actually very few questions were asked about how the historical documents, historical in the usual sense, were compiled and if they are capable of confirming a belief in the existence of Christ Jesus. Too much still lived in human souls that had radiated down from the working of the Mystery of Golgotha. People had been able to perceive for themselves, so to speak, only too clearly the influence proceeding from the name of Christ Jesus through the centuries for them to think it necessary to ask whether any document was extant capable of proving the existence of Christ Jesus. To those who professed Him in any way His existence was entirely self-evident; and more than is generally believed today it was just as self-evident that they ought to hold firmly to the belief in His being as both human and superhuman, and at the same time spiritual and divine.

However, as time went on materialism came into being, and with it something entered mankind's evolution that necessarily belongs to the materialistic point of view. The materialistic world conception cannot tolerate the idea that something like a higher individuality lives in man. It cannot accept the notion that one can penetrate behind the outer personality to something spiritual in man. If you look at human beings materialistically, and this happens most radically in our time, then from a materialistic viewpoint all human beings will appear to you to be much the same. They all walk on two legs, all have a head, and a nose situated at a particular point on the face, all have two eyes and a part of the head covered with hair, and so on. From this materialistic viewpoint all human beings look much the same. So why should this age look for anything behind the outer man? This idea seriously offends someone who cannot bring himself to admit that in his present incarnation there is within him something that is equally important also in other human beings. Materialism will not admit that. So the possibility was lost of understanding that the Christ could have lived within the man Jesus of Nazareth; and the more the eighteenth century wore on the more any idea at all of the Christ was lost. Attention was directed more and more toward Jesus of Nazareth, who must have been born in Nazareth or somewhere else, who lived like a man, doing nothing but proclaim fine principles and in some way or another may have died the death of a martyr. More and more the man Jesus replaced the Christ Jesus of earlier centuries. This, from the point of view of materialism, was a self-evident fact.

It was also entirely natural that in the course of the nineteenth century there should have developed what may be called "research into the life of Jesus." Enlightened theology also carries out research into the life of Jesus, that is to say, it tries to establish the facts about Jesus of Nazareth in just the same way as facts are established about Charlemagne, Otto the Great and similar personalities. However, it is very difficult to establish the facts about Jesus of Nazareth. In the first place all the principal documents that must come under consideration are the Gospels and the Pauline letters. But it is obvious that documents such as the Gospels cannot be counted as historical. There are four Gospels and from the external materialistic point of view they all contradict each other. All kinds of ways out of this dilemma have been sought in the course of "research into the life of Jesus." A certain phase of this research can first of all be disregarded. Because this research fell into the materialistic period there was no longer any desire to believe in miracles. As a result some of the miracles are explained in the most peculiar way, as for example the kind of interpretation that tried to explain the appearance of Christ Jesus on the lake by suggesting that He did not walk on the lake with physical feet—we have dealt with this story earlier—but the disciples were simply unaware of the physical laws of the world. One far-fetched explanation from this Jesus research suggested that the apostles went by ship while Christ Jesus was accompanying them on the shore and that the people on the opposite shore could easily have been mistaken and believed that Jesus was walking on the water! To say nothing of other peculiarities thought up by rationalists, for example that when water was transformed into wine something like a wine-essence was smuggled into the water! Someone actually tried to explain the baptism by John in the Jordan by saying that just at that moment a dove happened to fly by! All this does exist. You would scarcely believe what has been put forward on the basis of strict objective science. But we may entirely disregard these aberrations, and look instead at the kind of research which tried to look at the supersensible from a materialistic viewpoint, not being able to handle the supersensible. This research regarded the supersensible elements as simply ornamentation. It decided that if anyone cannot believe in Christ Jesus, nor that someone was born as a carpenter's son in Nazareth, was in the temple at the age of twelve and so on, nevertheless if everything supersensible is removed and if everything that harmonizes or does not harmonize in the various Gospels is combined, then it is possible to produce something like a biography of Jesus of Nazareth. The effort was made to do this in the most varied ways, but it was really inevitable that each biography was different when so many different people tried to write a biography of this kind. But we cannot enter here into such details. There was also a period when during this "research into the life of Jesus" it was supposed that Jesus of Nazareth was a superior human being, something not unlike a higher Socrates, higher in the sense attributed to that word by materialists.

Such was the kind of research into the life of Jesus of Nazareth whose principal aim was to create a biography of Jesus. However, such an effort was bound to give rise to criticism, especially on two counts, in the first place because of the documents themselves; for the Gospels are not documents at all in the sense that one speaks of historical documents, as they are evaluated by historians. This is primarily due to the many contradictions to be found in them and the way in which they have been preserved. Secondly, in recent years something new was added to this "research into the life of Jesus" because those who went deeply into certain passages in the Gospels discovered certain constantly recurring remarks, which, as you know, refer to supersensible facts. But these men, in spite of being in the clutches of materialism, when they found these things could not simply disregard them, as was done by the researchers into the life of Jesus. So they moved on to something different, to the "Christ research," which in recent years has come into prominence, by contrast with the "research into the life of Jesus," which culminated in the term coined by a present day professor: the "plain man from Nazareth." This was found very agreeable by many people; it was flattering to them not to have to recognize anything higher in the Gospels. It suited them better to speak of the "plain man from Nazareth" rather than to ascend to the "God-Man."

Then the God-Man was really found, and there followed "research into Christ." This was a most peculiar phenomenon, appearing in an especially grotesque form in the work *Ecce Deus* of Benjamin Smith, and in other works by the same author. The attempt was made to prove that Jesus of Nazareth never really existed; he is only a legend. Nevertheless, the Gospels give an account of Jesus Christ. What is this Jesus Christ? Well, he is a fictional God, an ideal image. From this point of view it is certainly not unreasonable to deny the real Jesus of Nazareth, for the Gospels speak of Christ and they attribute to Him qualities that, according to materialistic interpretations, do not exist. Then evidence follows that He cannot have existed historically, so He must be fictional, a fiction that originated in the period assigned to the Mystery of Golgotha. So there has been a kind of return from Jesus to Christ in recent years. But Christ is in no sense real; He lives only in human thoughts. So we may say that everything in this realm today rests without solid foundations.

Naturally the general public does not know much about the things that are happening in this realm. Everything connected with the Mystery of Golgotha has been totally undermined on scientific grounds; there is no longer any firm foundation. The "research into the life of Jesus" has collapsed because it can prove nothing, and the "Christ research" is not worth even discussing. The crucial point is the tremendous effect that emanates from that being with whom the Mystery of Golgotha is linked. If the whole thing is a fiction, then this materialistic age should agree to cease to look at it as soon as possible, for a materialistic age cannot believe in a "fiction" that is supposed nevertheless to have fulfilled the most important mission of all time! Yes, our enlightened age has surely been successful in accumulating contradictions, and is scarcely aware how much it is in need, just in the scientific field, of the saying, "Lord, forgive them for they know not what they do." This indeed is equally applicable to all current research regarding Jesus and Christ which has no wish to place itself in a serious and dignified way on a spiritual base.

The Gospel itself clearly points to what has appeared in our time in the manner just described. Those people who wish to remain materialists and to believe in nothing whatever beyond what can be attained by materialistic consciousness based on sense perception can find no path leading to Christ Jesus. For this path has been closed because those who stood closest to Christ left Him just at the time the Mystery of Golgotha was taking place. It was only later that they met Him again, thus failing to participate in what happened in Palestine on the physical plane. And everyone knows for certain that no credible documents have been furnished by the other side of the threshold. Yet in the Mark Gospel and in the other Gospels descriptions of this very Mystery of Golgotha have been given.

How then did these descriptions come into being? It is of the utmost importance for us to picture this to ourselves. Let us consider the descriptions given in one instance, in the Gospel of St. Mark. Even though the description is short and concise, it is in fact indicated to us quite adequately how after the scene of the Resurrection the youth in the white garment, that is to say, the cosmic Christ, again showed

Himself to the disciples after the Mystery had been accomplished, and gave certain impulses to them. As a consequence the apostles, among whom we should include Peter, could be enkindled to clairvoyant vision, so that afterward they could see clairvoyantly what they had been unable to see with their physical eyes because they fled. The eyes of Peter, and of others who were permitted to be their pupils after the Resurrection of Christ Jesus, were opened clairvoyantly so that they could through clairvoyance behold the Mystery of Golgotha.

Although the Mystery of Golgotha took place on the physical plane, the only path to it is that of clairvoyance; and we must keep this firmly in our minds. The Gospel points this out quite clearly when it tells us how those who had been summoned fled at the decisive moment, so that it was only after it had received the impulse of the Risen One that in such a soul as that of Peter the memory flashed up of what had happened after the flight. In ordinary life man remembers only what he has experienced in sense existence. The kind of clairvoyance that now appeared in the disciples differs from ordinary memory in that they were able to remember physical material events, just as if these events had been in their memories, although they were not present. Just imagine how memory shone forth in the soul of a man like Peter, when he remembered events at which he had not been directly present. And so Peter, for example, taught those who wished to hear him about the Mystery of Golgotha, *from memory*, taught them what he *remembered*, even though he had not been present.

It was in this way that the teachings, the revelations about the Mystery of Golgotha came into being. But the impulse that emanated from the Christ to such disciples as Peter could also be communicated to those who were pupils of these disciples. The man who originally compiled, even though in an oral form, the Gospel called the Gospel of St.

187

Mark, was just such a pupil of Peter. So the impulse that had manifested itself in Peter himself passed into the soul of Mark, with the result that within Mark's own soul there flashed up what had been accomplished in Jerusalem as the Mystery of Golgotha. Mark remained a pupil of Peter for some time. Then he came to an area where he truly had the external milieu, so to speak, the outer environment which enabled him to give the particular coloring needed for this Gospel.

Through all that we have presented to you—and perhaps in the future it will be possible to say more on the subject— one thing has been shown in particular: that the Mark Gospel allows us to feel most clearly the whole cosmic greatness and significance of Christ. It was possible for the original author of this Gospel to be stimulated to give his description of the cosmic greatness of Christ precisely because of the place to which he had moved after he had been Peter's pupil. He moved to Alexandria in Egypt and lived there at a period when in a certain way Jewish-philosophical-theosophical learning in Alexandria had reached a certain culmination. He could take up in Alexandria what at that time were the best aspects of pagan gnosis. He could absorb views that were also in existence there about how the human being has come forth from the spiritual, and how he came into contact with Lucifer and Ahriman, and how luciferic and ahrimanic forces are taken up into the human soul. From the pagan gnosis he could accept everything that was told him about the origin of man out of the cosmos when our planet came into being. But Mark could also see, especially when he was living in an Egyptian locality, how strong the contrast was between what had originally been destined for man, and what he had by this time become.

This was shown most strikingly in Egyptian culture, which had originated from the loftiest revelations that had then become manifest in Egyptian architecture, especially in the pyramids and palaces, in the culture of the Sphinx, which, however was falling ever more into corruption and decadence. Thus it was particularly the greatest works of Egyptian culture that sank down, still during the third cultural epoch, into the worst aberrations of black magic, and the worst depravities of spiritual corruption. If one had the spiritual eyes for it, it was possible in a certain way to see in what was practised in Egypt the most profound secrets because this culture emanated from the pure original Hermes wisdom. But only a soul that looked at the foundation, and not at the existing corruption, could see this. Already by the time of Moses corruption was far advanced, and he had to extract from Egyptian culture the good which was scarcely visible even to such a noble soul as Moses. It could then be passed on indirectly to posterity through the soul of Moses. Thereafter the corruption in Egypt continued unabated.

Mark's soul was alive to the possibility that mankind could sink down and become engulfed in materialism, especially in regard to its view of the world. And he experienced in particular one thing that men can again today experience in a different, though in some respects similar, form—though only by men who possess the necessary feeling and perception. For we are really today experiencing the reemergence of Egyptian culture. I have often emphasized the peculiar nature of these linkages between cultures in human evolution, and I have explained how among the seven successive cultural epochs of the post-Atlantean era the fourth cultural epoch that contains Hellenism and the Mystery of Golgotha stands by itself. However, the third cultural epoch, that of the Egypto-Chaldean culture, emerges once more, though in an unspiritual manner, in the culture, especially the science of today. Within our materialistic culture, even in its outer manifestations, we have in this fifth age a certain reawakening of the culture of the third epoch. In a certain way the second will also reappear in the sixth and the first in the seventh. So do these spans of time encircle and include each other, as we have often emphasized. Today we are experiencing something that a spirit like Mark could experience in a most intensive way.

If we consider the culture of today, we should not describe it in this way to the outside world because it could not bear it; even if we overlook the most radical forms of corruption we can still say that everything is mechanized. And within our materialistic culture it is only mechanism that is worshipped, even if we do not call it prayer or devotion. It is true that our soul forces that in former times were directed toward spiritual beings are now directed only toward machines, toward mechanisms. One can truly say that they receive the attention that once was given to the gods. This is especially the case in the realm of science, this science which is totally unaware of how little it is concerned with truth, with real truth, and at the same time how little it is concerned with true logic. If we look at it from a higher point of view we can certainly say that there is today a deeply serious and intense striving, an intense longing. I spoke already in Munich (in August, 1912, Ed.) in a lecture about the longing in our time, and especially how this longing has taken root in individual souls. But in present day "official" science such a longing is missing, and instead one might say that there is a certain satisfied contentment. Yet this contentment has something strange about it, since it is a contentment with what is unreal and illogical. Nowhere is this science capable of recognizing how deeply it is entrenched in what is opposed to all logic. All this can easily be seen and experienced, and it is indeed true that in human evolution one pole must be enkindled by the other. It is the very inadequacy of external science and its unreality and illogicality, the way it prides itself on its knowledge and its total unawareness of its deficiencies, that will and must gradually give rise to the noblest

190

reaction within human souls: the longing for the spiritual that is manifesting itself in our time.

For a long time still to come people who remain attached to this unreality and lack of logic may well make fun of spiritual science, will scoff at it, or label it dangerous in all sorts of ways. Nevertheless through the inner power of the facts themselves the other pole will be enkindled, entirely of its own accord. And if those who understand something of it would only refrain from relapsing into the sickness of compromises and were to see clearly, then the time might well come much more quickly than seems likely now. For again and again it is our experience that if a learned man turns up and says something that someone else thinks is "quite anthroposophical," then a great fuss is immediately made of it. More so still if someone or other preaches from a pulpit something that is thought to be "quite anthroposophical." What is important is not that such compromises are made, but that we should place ourselves clearly and sincerely in the spiritual life, and allow it to affect us through its own impulses. The more clearly we are aware that the inner vitality of spiritual life must be enkindled, and the more we become convinced that we have no right to accept from the materialistic thinking of our time anything that is not well grounded in fact, the better it will be. This is a very different thing from demonstrating that truly progressive science is in harmony with spiritual research.

It can be shown how at every step science commits logical blunders on every page of its literary works, of the kind often referred to by one of our friends in a humorous manner. A certain Professor Schlaucherl ("clever fellow") a character in the comic paper *Fliegender Blätter* wished to prove just how a frog hears. To this end the Professor causes the frog to jump on a table, then he hits the top of the table. The frog jumps away, thus proving he heard the tap. Then he proceeds to tear off the frog's legs, and again hits the table. But this time the frog does not jump away, proving clearly that the frog hears with his legs. For when he still had legs he jumped away, but when he had lost his legs he no longer jumped. Learned men do indeed make all kinds of experiments with frogs. But in other domains their logical inferences are just like this example, as, for instance, in their much lauded brain research. Attention is drawn to the fact that words can be remembered and certain thoughts may be produced if this or that part of the brain is present. But if this part of the brain is missing then words can no longer be remembered nor is it possible to have thoughts—exactly the same logic as in the case of the frog who hears through his legs. Indeed there are no better grounds for saying that a man can think with one part of his brain or cannot think if this part of the brain is missing, than there are for saying that the frog can no longer hear when his legs have been torn off. The two cases are entirely parallel, only people do not notice that the whole inference rests on nothing but faulty reasoning. We could continue to point out faulty reasoning piled on more faulty reasoning in all the results of what science believes to be firmly established. And the more mistakes that are made the more proud people are of science, and the more they scoff at spiritual science.

This will have the result of generating the noblest of reactions, a longing for spiritual science. Such a reaction that belongs to our era is the same as what must have been experienced by Mark in his own age when he was able to perceive how mankind had descended from its former spiritual height and had become enmeshed in materialism. Through this experience he gained a profound understanding of how the greatest impulse lives in the supersensible, and this understanding was further strengthened by his teacher. What Peter had given him regarding the Mystery of Golgotha was not something that could have been based on sense perception and then handed down by tradition, as if someone had seen with his own eyes what had happened at Jerusalem. The events described were investigated later through clairvoyance; and it is in this way that all information about Christ Jesus and the Mystery of Golgotha was gained.

The Mystery of Golgotha is an event that occurred on the physical plane, but it could be seen afterward only through clairvoyance. I want you to bear in mind most particularly that the Mystery of Golgotha is a physical-material event, but the path leading toward understanding it must nevertheless be looked for in a superphysical, supersensible way and in spite of the documents that have come down to us. People who do not understand this may argue about the merits of this or that Gospel. But for one who is aware of the true state of affairs, such questions do not exist. Such a one knows how necessary it is for us to look beyond the often imperfect traditions represented by the various Gospels, and reach what clairvoyant investigation alone can tell us today. And if we investigate the truth of what actually happened by reconstructing it with the aid of the Akasha Chronicle, then we shall see how we must interpret the Gospels and what we have to read in individual passages. We shall see how we must read about what was then placed before humanity as man's true dignity, his true being, at a time when mankind had descended most deeply from its former heights.

The divine spiritual powers have given to man his outer image, his outer form. But since the old Lemurian epoch what lived in this outer form stood always under the influence of the luciferic forces, and then, during the later phases of evolution also under the ahrimanic forces. It was under these influences that what men have called science, knowledge and understanding have come into being. It is no wonder that just exactly at that time the true supersensible being of man appeared before mankind, and men were least able to recognize it, and were least able to know what mankind

193

had become. Man's knowledge and understanding had become ever more deeply enmeshed in sense existence, and gradually became ever less capable of penetrating close to the true being of man.

This is the important point we must take into consideration when we turn again to the forsaken Son of Man, to the form of the man who stands before us at the moment when, according to the Mark Gospel, the cosmic Christ was only loosely connected with the Son of Man. There, before all humanity, stood the man, the man in the form originally given to man by divine spiritual powers. There He stood, but ennobled and spiritualized by the three-year sojourn of the Christ within the body of Jesus of Nazareth. Here He stood before His fellow-men. But man's understanding had reached only as far as was possible through the thousands of years during which Lucifer and Ahriman had penetrated his understanding and knowing. Yet here stood the man who in those three years had driven out of Himself the influences of Lucifer and Ahriman. Here in front of other men stood restored what man had been before the coming of Lucifer and Ahriman. Only through the impulse of the cosmic Christ was man once again what he had been when he left the spiritual world and was brought down into the physical world. Here stood the spirit of mankind, the Son of Man, in the presence of men who at that time were the judges and executioners in Jerusalem. He stood there in the form that man can become if all that has debased him were to be driven out from his nature. Here stood the man at the moment when the Mystery of Golgotha was being accomplished, in the image of His fellowmen. Before such a man His fellowmen should have stood and worshipped, saying, "Here am I in my true nature, here is my highest ideal. Here am I, in the form to which I can attain only through my most ardent striving, a striving that can come only from the depths of my soul. Here I stand before that in myself which is alone worthy of reverence and worship, the divine in me.'' And the apostles, if they had been able to practice self-knowledge, would have been compelled to say, ''In the whole expanse of space there is nothing in existence that can be compared in greatness with what is before us in the Son of Man!''

At that moment in history mankind ought to have possessed that self-knowledge. But what did this mankind do? It spat upon the Son of Man, it scourged Him, and led Him forth to the place of execution. That was the dramatic turning point between what ought to have been, the recognition that something was there with which nothing in the world is comparable, and what was described as actually happening. Instead of recognizing himself, man is described as having crushed himself under foot, as having killed himself because he did not recognize himself. Yet through this lesson, this cosmic lesson he is able to receive the impulse to attain gradually for himself his true being within the wider perspective of earth evolution!

This therefore was the world-historical moment, and this is the way we must characterize it if we want to do so in the right way entirely in accord with the powerful, striking sentences of the Gospel of St. Mark. It not only needs to be understood, it needs to be *felt*, sensed. Out of this crushing under foot of man's own nature there came forth what was described in my lecture cycle *From Jesus to Christ* in Karlsruhe as the ''phantom.'' Because man crushed his own being under foot, that which was the outer image of the divine was transformed into the phantom which multiplies, and multiplying during the further development of mankind is able to penetrate into the souls of men, as was described in the Karlsruhe cycle.

If we look at things in this way, then the great difference becomes visible between what the Mark Gospel really wishes to describe, and what is so often made of it today. Anyone who understands a Gospel, and particularly the Mark Gospel, in such a way that he can sense and feel what is described in accordance with its artistic composition and its deep content, will have the experience that this feeling will become a true inner fact, the kind of inner fact that must be present if we wish to attain to a relationship with Christ Jesus. The soul must really dedicate itself, at least in some small measure, to the kind of reflection filled with feeling and emotion that can arise from a reading of the Mark Gospel and that may be characterized somewhat as follows, "How greatly deluded were my fellowmen who stood around the Son of Man, when in truth they should have perceived there the highest ideal of themselves!"

A typical man of this materialistic age may write down or let slip such a remark as can often be heard or read today, especially from superstitious monists, I mean enlightened monists, "Why is existence as it is? Why do we suffer pain? These questions no one has ever been able to answer. Buddha, Christ, Socrates, Giordano Bruno, none of them have been able to lift a corner of this veil." People who write in this way do not realize that in so doing they are placing themselves much higher than Buddha, Christ, Socrates and the rest, nor that they in working on this assumption understand everything. How could it be otherwise in an age when any beginning university lecturer possesses an unrivalled understanding of everything that has happened in history, and is obliged for the sake of his career to write books on the subject?

It might be thought that this is said out of a desire to criticize our age. This is not the reason. But such things ought to be visible to our souls because only if we allow them to be perceived by our souls do we keep a true perspective on the overpowering greatness of the Gospels, as, for instance, the Gospel of St. Mark. These things are constantly misunderstood for no other reason than that people can approach such a height only slowly, and usually only caricatures are presented to them. In every detail the Gospels are great, and in essence every detail teaches us something extraordinary.

We can therefore learn something also from the last chapter of the Mark Gospel. Of course if I were to point out all the great thoughts in this Gospel I should have to go on speaking for a long time yet. But one such detail immediately at the beginning of the sixteenth chapter shows us how deeply the evangelist has penetrated into the secrets of existence. So the author of the Mark Gospel knew, as we have described, how humanity had declined, sinking from the spiritual heights into materialism. He knew how little human beings were truly able to grasp the nature of the being of man, and how little people at the time of the Mystery of Golgotha were capable of understanding what happened then.

At this point I should like to remind you of something I have often pointed out with regard to the difference between male and female, pointing out the fact that to some extent the female element—not the single individual woman but rather "womanhood"—has not entirely descended to the physical plane, whereas the man—again not a single individuality, not man in a particular incarnation but "manhood" —has crossed the line and descended lower. As a result true humanity lies between man and woman; and it is for this reason that a human being also changes sex in different incarnations. But it is already the case that the woman, as such, because of the different formation of her brain and the different way in which she can use it, is able to grasp spiritual ideas with greater facility. By contrast the man because of his external physical corporeality is much better adapted to think himself into materialism, because, if we wish to express the matter crudely, his brain is harder. The female brain is softer, not so stubborn, that is to say in general—I am not referring to individual personalities. In the case of individual personalities there is no need to flatter oneself,

for many truly obstinate heads sit on many a female body—
to say nothing of the reverse! But on the whole it is true that
it is easier to make use of a female brain if one is to understand something exceptional, as long as the will to do so is
also present. It is for this reason that the evangelist after the
Mystery of Golgotha allows women to appear first.

> And now, as the Sabbath was over, Mary Magdalene and
> Mary the mother of James, and Salome, brought spices, so
> that they could go and anoint him. (Mark 16: 1.)

And it was to them that the youth, that is, the cosmic
Christ, first appeared; and only afterward to the male disciples. True occultism, true spiritual science is interwoven
into the composition and details of the contents of the Gospels, and especially of the concise Mark Gospel.

Only if we feel what speaks to us from the Gospels and
allow ourselves to be stirred by what we feel and sense can
we find the way to the Mystery of Golgotha. And then there
will be no longer any question as to whether these Gospels
are genuine or false from the external historical point of
view. Those who understand nothing of the matter can be
left to their investigations. But those who ascend by means
of spiritual science to a feeling for and understanding of the
Gospels will gradually realize that they are not in the first
place intended to be historical documents but rather documents that flow into our souls. And when they pour out
their impulses into our souls, then our souls, without the aid
of any documents, are taken hold of by what they feel and
experience when they turn their gaze to the Mystery of Golgotha, and recognize how human understanding, knowledge
and cognition when directed to the being of man have fallen
short—how men spat on and crucified this being of man that
they should have revered in the wisdom of self-knowledge
as their highest ideal. And from this recognition the soul
will win for itself the supreme strength needed to rise up-

ward to the ideal that radiates across from Golgotha and shines upon all who are willing to feel and perceive it. For only then will men truly grasp the reality that the earth is linked with the spiritual worlds, when they understand how the spiritual reality, the Christ, lived as a cosmic being in the body of Jesus of Nazareth; and when they understand that all the leaders of humanity that the world has ever known were sent out by the Christ as His forerunners with the task of preparing the way for Him so that He could be recognized and understood. All this preparation turned out to be virtually useless when the Mystery of Golgotha took place, for at the decisive moment everything failed. But ever more and more in the future the time will come when people will understand not only the Mystery of Golgotha itself but all the other events that accompanied it, by means of which the Mystery will be ever more fully understood.

For the time being the peoples of Europe can easily per-haps be misjudged because they do not act like many other peoples who recognize as the true religion only those reli-gious creeds that have sprung from their own nation and race, as for example, in India in particular, where only that is considered valuable that has sprung from their own blood. How often in theosophical circles one talks about how the equality of all religions ought to be recognized, whereas in reality one wishes only to promote one's own religion and looks upon that as the only real wisdom-reli-gion. The Europeans are totally unable to do this because not a single people of Europe has retained any national deity, any deity growing out of its own soil of the kind that the peoples of Asia possess. Christ Jesus belongs to Asia, and the peoples of Europe have adopted Him, and allowed Him to influence them. In the acceptance of Christ Jesus there is no egoism; and it would be a complete distortion if someone were to wish to compare the way a European speaks about Christ Jesus with the way other peoples speak about their national deities, for example the way a Chinese speaks about Confucious or the way an Indian speaks about Krishna or the Buddha.

And we can speak of Christ Jesus from a purely objective historical standpoint. This objective history is concerned with nothing else but the great appeal to man's self-knowledge, a self-knowledge that was so completely distorted into its opposite while the Mystery of Golgotha was taking place. Yet through this Mystery the possibility was given to man to receive the impulse to find his own true being, whereas, as far as knowledge, external knowledge, was concerned, humanity totally failed to grasp the meaning of the Mystery of Golgotha, as we have seen. And so all the world's religions will one day rightly understand each other and work together to understand what the Mystery of Golgotha contains, and to make its impulse accessible to men.

If it is once realized that when Christ Jesus is spoken of this has nothing to do with any egoistic creed, but with something that, as a historical fact in human evolution, can belong to every religious creed, then, and then only, will the kernel of wisdom and truth in all religions be grasped. And to the extent to which we still do not accept spiritual science in its true sense, it is to the same extent that we refuse to accept the true understanding of the Mystery of Golgotha. And to the extent that we understand spiritual science, it is to that extent that a human being can understand the Mystery of Golgotha. So a Christian who accepts spiritual science can really come to an understanding with all the peoples of the world. And if representatives of other religions with a somewhat excessive, though understandable and even justifiable pride were to say, "You Christians have only one single incarnation of God, but we can offer several, and thus are richer than you," no Christian should try to rival him by claiming something similar for Christ Jesus, since this would show his lack of understanding for the

200

Mystery of Golgotha. The correct thing would be for a Christian to say in reply to someone who is able to show that the founder of his own religion had many incarnations, "Yes, of course, but all those who had many incarnations could not have fulfilled the Mystery of Golgotha. Look where you will, in no other religion will you ever find it in the way it is presented in Christianity."

On other occasions in the past I have already shown how, if we follow the life of the Buddha we shall reach the point described in the Mark Gospel as the scene of the Transfiguration of Christ. At this point the Buddha's life has come to its final end, and he dissolves into light, as it is described, and this description in truth corresponds to the occult fact. In the case of Christ, as you will find it stated in *Christianity as Mystical Fact*, He does indeed reach the scene of the Transfiguration. But He was not transfigured alone, by Himself; He converses with Moses and Elijah on the mountain, where cosmic events occur. *Only after the scene of the Transfiguration does the Mystery of Golgotha begin.* This emerges so clearly from the documents themselves that it is fundamentally impossible to deny the fact, once one has recognized it from a comparison between the lives of Christ and the Buddha. And in essence all that I was able to tell you today about the feelings that arise in us when we think of the great misunderstanding of the Son of Man by human beings is only a consequence of what you will find already pointed out in *Christianity as Mystical Fact*.

And now, at the conclusion of our studies on the Mark Gospel I may in a certain respect say that the program laid down at the beginning of the anthroposophical movement in Central Europe insofar as it related to Christianity has in all essentials been completed in every detail. When we started, our main task was to show how in the course of time religions have developed, culminating in the problem of Christ. We have considered the individual Gospels and various cosmic revelations; we have tried to penetrate ever more deeply into the depths of occult life in order to carry out what we indicated we should do at the beginning. We have tried to work consistently, but in essence all we have done is complete in detail what we said we would do when we started. Was this not the most natural development with respect to the Christ problem within the theosophical movement of Central Europe? In view of all this that has happened, other people who became converts to an impossible conception of Christ within the framework of Christianity can scarcely demand that we who have done this consistent work for years should be converts to their conception of Christ devised three years ago! It has often been emphasized of recent years that the Theosophical Society ought to be hospitable to all opinions. Of course it should be. But the matter appears in a quite different light if it is to be hospitable to the successive different opinions of the same personality, if that personality now maintains something different from what it did four years ago, and now demands that the Theosophical Society should provide a home for this latest opinion. Such a thing may be possible, but there is no need for us to go along with it. Nor should one be considered a heretic if one doesn't take part in such things. In Central Europe people go further still, going so far as to call white black and black white!

This is indeed a solemn moment when we are bringing to an end the latest and final phase of the work we have been carrying on for the last ten years according to plan. So we are determined to stand firm in this work and neither become discouraged nor yet lacking in understanding for others. But we must see very clearly what we have to do, and we must stand firm on our own ground and not allow ourselves to be discouraged by anything, even if white is called black and black white. Even if our anthroposophical Central European movement—in which everyone strives to do his best according to his ability, and everyone is called upon to give his best without submitting to any authority—is said to be full of fanatics and dogmatizers, we should still not be discouraged, not even if those who have their own dogma that is scarcely three years old try to organize an opposition to the dreadful dogma of Central Europe. It is painful to witness the kind of mischievous tricks that are played today in the name of Christ. We are justified in using words like these, and regard them as nothing more than a technical term, used objectively. We are doing nothing more than stating the actual fact, without emotion and without criticism. If we are obliged to put it this way it is the fault of the objective fact itself.

But these facts, when they are set against what can flow to us from a real understanding of the Gospel of St. Mark, can also lead to no other course than to continue to work in the way we have recognized as the right one. This has proved itself in our general program based on positive facts, and continues to prove itself again every day as long as we apply it to individual problems and individual facts. And as we make our way step by step through the details of the things we have to investigate, what was said at the beginning is invariably confirmed. So even when we are studying the loftiest things we can harbor no other feeling than a true and genuine feeling for truth. Such things as the contemplation of the Mystery of Golgotha have within them already the necessary healing power that dispels error if we approach them in the spirit. Then we are led to recognize how in essence it is only an insufficient will to pursue the truth that prevents us from truly pursuing the path that opens out from the earthly into the cosmic, when the cosmic Christ within Jesus of Nazareth is investigated. But He appears to us so clearly if we understand a work like the Mark Gospel.

For this reason such works, after they have been opened up to the understanding of men by means of spiritual scientific studies, will gradually also reach out to the rest of mankind, and will be ever more clearly understood. And attention will be focused ever more on the words of the Gospels rediscovered without the aid of sense perception through clairvoyant vision of the Mystery of Golgotha. Those who wrote the Gospels from clairvoyant observation described the physical events afterward. This must be understood, as also the necessity for it. Those people who lived at the same time as the events in Palestine were incapable of understanding what happened at that time because it was only through the impulse given by this event that it could be understood! Before the event had taken place no one was alive who could have understood it. It had first to take effect, so it could be understood only after the event. The key to the understanding of this Mystery of Golgotha is the Mystery of Golgotha itself! Christ had first to do all that He had to do up to the time of the Mystery of Golgotha, and only through the effects of what He did could the understanding of Himself come forth. Then through what He was, the Word could be enkindled which is at the same time the expression of His true being.

And so through what Christ was, the primal Word is enkindled which is communicated to us and can be recognized again in clairvoyant vision, this Word which also proclaims the true being of the Mystery of Golgotha. We may also think of this Word when we speak of Christ's own words, not only those that He spoke Himself but those which He also kindled in the souls of those able to understand Him, so that they could both understand and describe His being from within their human souls.

As long as the earth endures men will take up into themselves the impulses from the Mystery of Golgotha. Then there will come an interval between "Earth" and "Jupiter." Such an interval is always linked to the fact that not only the individual planet, but all its surroundings change, pass into chaos, undergo a "pralaya." And not only the earth itself will be different in *pralaya*, but also the heavens belonging to the earth. But what has been given to the earth through the Word that Christ spoke, which He kindled also in those who recognize Him, is the true essence of earth existence. And a right understanding allows us to recognize the truth of that saying that tells us of the development of the cosmos, how the earth and heaven as seen from the earth will be different after the earth has reached its goal, and heaven and earth pass away. But such a Word as could be spoken by Christ about heaven and earth will remain. If one rightly understands the Gospels, and feels their innermost impulse, then one feels not only the truth but also the power of the Word which as power passes over into us, enabling us to gaze out beyond the wide world as we take up into ourselves with full understanding the Word, "Heaven and Earth shall pass away, but my words shall not pass away." (Matt. 24: 35.)

The words of Christ will never pass away, even if heaven and earth pass away. This may be said in accordance with occult knowledge, for the truths of the Mystery of Golgotha that have been spoken will still remain. The Mark Gospel kindles in our souls the knowledge of the truth that heaven and earth pass away, while what we can know about the Mystery of Golgotha will accompany us into the ages that are to come, even if heaven and earth will have passed away!

Note on the Translation

This vital but difficult cycle has been published twice before in English, the first in an edition of 1923 published by Harry Collison, and the other published in 1950 by the Anthroposophic Press in New York. These two editions were based on two different German versions. Both these earlier translations had many virtues, but the two translators were inclined to gloss over some of the difficulties in the text, and their interpretations were often at variance with one another. It was therefore decided to commission another translation altogether which would be more literal and more faithful to Steiner's words as printed in the latest German edition of 1976 (GA 139). It is this translation by Conrad Mainzer that has been mainly used for the present edition, although many changes had to be made in it in order to make it acceptable to English speaking readers. The result is therefore a wholly new translation, even when the wording of one or the other of the earlier translators has been adopted; and every effort has been made by the editor to make this new publication worthy of the content of this, the last and most profound of Steiner's cycles of the four Gospels.

The biblical quotations may not sound familiar to readers who have always favored the King James Version, the version used in the two earlier English translations. For the most part the translations are those made by Conrad Mainzer from Steiner's wording, though in a few instances they have been revised to bring them into conformity with the original Greek. Though unfamiliar it is hoped they will prove acceptable and more easily comprehensible than the often archaic language of the earlier versions.

Notes

1 : 3 Giotto di Bondone (c. 1266–1337), Florentine painter and architect, noted especially for his frescoes on the life of St. Francis.

Dante Alighieri, 1265–1321, Italian poet, author of the *Divine Comedy*.

1 : 4 David, second king of Israel, ruled about the beginning of the first millennium B.C. Many of the most beautiful Psalms were attributed to him, and it was their influence of which Rudolf Steiner was evidently thinking in this passage.

Homer, Greek poet who lived probably in the 8th century B.C., author of the *Iliad* and the *Odyssey*.

Goethe, Johann Wolfgang von, 1749–1832. German poet, author of *Faust*.

1 : 5 Schopenhauer, Artur, 1788–1860. German philosopher, author of *The World as Will and Idea*.

Hartmann, Eduard von, German philosopher, author of *The Philosophy of the Unconscious* (1842–1906).

1 : 7 Ram Mohan Roy, 1772–1836, founder of the Brahmo Samaj.

Tagore, Rabindranath, 1861–1941. Indian poet and philosopher, winner of Nobel Prize for Literature, 1913.

One of these followers—reference is to Keshab Chandra Sen, 1834–1884.

1 : 12　Empedocles of Agragas, c. 495–435 B.C., Greek philosopher.

2 : 22　The two books of the Maccabees are to be found in the Apocrypha, but not in the King James Version of the Bible. The heroic deeds of Judas Maccabaeus are recorded in Book 1, and the story of the martyrdom of the sons of the widow in Book 2.

3 : 46　Raphael. Raffaello Santi, 1483–1520, Italian painter, famous especially for his Madonnas and for his paintings in the Stanza della Segnatura in the Vatican, especially The School of Athens and the Disputà.

3 : 46　. . . proof to which I already alluded in Munich. In a lecture of August 31, 1912, not translated, entitled, "Theosophy and the Spiritual Life of the Present."

3 : 47　Hermann Grimm, 1828–1901. The books on Raphael written by him appeared under the title *Das Leben Raphael* (The Life of Raphael) 1872, 1885 and 1896. *Raphael als Weltmacht* (Raphael as World Power) appears in his posthumously published *Fragments*, Vol. II.

4 : 66　Socrates, Athenian philosopher, 470–399 B.C. Our information about him comes mainly from the works of Plato and Xenophon, the more sympathetic and much better known picture being drawn from Plato. Socrates is not known ever to have written a word, his instruction having been all given orally, in the form of dialogues.

Plato's picture of Socrates is contained mostly in his Protagoras, Meno, Symposium, Gorgias, and the three dialogues recounting the death of Socrates: The Apology, the Crito, and the Phaedo. Plato, 427–347 B.C.

Aristotle, 384–322 B.C. A pupil of Plato, he never knew Socrates personally, but credits him with many philosophical innovations, especially the use of logic and dialectic.

4 : 70   Gautama Buddha, c. 563–483 B.C. His dialogue with his pupil Sona is recorded in *Vinayapitaka* I, page 182 in the edition of H. Oldenberg (in German).

5 : 83   Krishna is usually regarded as a mythical figure, and a member of the Hindu pantheon, one of the earthly avatars, or incarnations of the god Vishnu. He appeared as the charioteer in the Hindu poem the *Bhagavad Gita*, in which he is endowed with divine attributes. Rudolf Steiner does not date his incarnation exactly, but gives it as occurring in the third post-Atlantean cultural epoch, which lasted from approximately 3000 B.C. to 747 B.C.

5 : 85   Fichte, Johann Gottlieb, 1762–1814. German idealist philosopher.

Schelling, Friedrich Wilhelm Joseph, 1775–1854. German idealist philosopher.

Hegel, Georg Wilhelm Friedrich, 1770–1831. Extremely influential German philosopher, professor at Berlin for many years. His *Encyclopaedia of the Philosophical Sciences in Outline* referred to by Steiner appeared in 1817.

5 : 90   *Knowledge of the Higher Worlds and its Attainment*, originally written in 1904 and published in the magazine *Luzifer-Gnosis*, has appeared in many editions in English, including the latest which appeared from Anthroposophic Press in 1984.

6 :108   Sinnet, A.P., 1840–1921. His *Esoteric Buddhism* was published in London in 1883, and a German translation appeared the following year.

7 :125   Rudolf Steiner gave his cycle on the Matthew Gospel in Bern in September, 1910. The last edition of this cycle in English was published in London by Rudolf Steiner Press in 1965. The question about the handing over of the power of the keys was discussed in Lectures 11 and 12.

7 :134   The lecture given by Michael Bauer was entitled "How did Hegel see the great Turning-Point in Time?" Among Hegel's more important works was his *Philosophy of History*.

7 :137   Pherecydes of Syros, 6th century B.C. Only fragments of his cosmogony have been preserved. For this reason and the "unphilosophical" nature of these fragments his name does not even appear in most histories of philosophy.

7 :138   Thales, Anaximander, Anaximenes (c. 636–546 B.C.; c. 611–547 B.C.; 6th century B.C.) were all from Miletus in Asia Minor and are regarded as the first true philosophers, Thales being, as Aristotle called him, the Father of Philosophy.

Heraclitus of Ephesus, c. 535–c. 475 B.C. Rudolf Steiner who discusses him at length in *Christianity as Mystical Fact* calls him an initiate priest as well as a philosopher.

Nietzsche, Friedrich, 1844–1900. German philosopher, author of *The Birth of Tragedy*, and *Thus Spake Zarathustra*.

Parmenides of Elea, born about 514 B.C., who held that true change was impossible and all apparent change was illusory.

Anaxagoras of Clazomenae, c. 500–428 B.C. Philosopher who is credited with founding the study of philosophy in Athens.

210

8 :149   Moses was discussed by Steiner in two of the earlier Gospel cycles, The Gospel of Luke (1909) and The Gospel of Matthew (1910). An important lecture was devoted to him on March 9, 1911. This appeared in *Turning Points in Spiritual History* (London, 1934).

10 :185   Benjamin Smith (1850–1912). His book *Ecce Deus*, which appeared in German in 1912 bore the subtitle, "The Early Christian Doctrine of the Purely-Divine Jesus."

10 :195   The cycle *From Jesus to Christ* was given in Karlsruhe in October, 1911. The lectures especially concerned with the phantom are six, seven and eight.

10 :201   *Christianity as Mystical Fact* consists of a series of lectures given in Berlin in 1902 and revised by Steiner for publication in the same year and again in 1910. The chapter entitled "Egyptian Mystery Wisdom" contains the statement about the Transfiguration to which he refers here. Available in English in three different translations.

FOR FURTHER READING

BASIC BOOKS

THEOSOPHY, AN INTRODUCTION TO THE SUPER-SENSIBLE KNOWLEDGE OF THE WORLD AND THE DESTINATION OF MAN
by Rudolf Steiner

In this work Steiner carefully explains many of the basic concepts and terminologies of anthroposophy. The book begins with a sensitive description of the fundamental trichotomy: body, soul, and spirit, elaborating the various higher members of the human constitution. A discussion of reincarnation and karma follows. The next and longest chapter (75 pages) presents, in a vast panorama, the seven regions of the soul world, the seven regions of the land of spirits, and the soul's journey after death through these worlds. A brief discussion of the path to higher knowledge follows.

"Read . . . Rudolf Steiner's little book on theosophy — your hair will stand on end!" Saul Bellow in **Newsweek**

(395 pp)	0-91014-239-4	Paper, $6.95 #155
	0-91014-265-3	Cloth, $14.00 #154

AN OUTLINE OF OCCULT SCIENCE *by Rudolf Steiner*

This lengthy work begins with a thorough discussion and definition of the term "occult science." A description of the supersensible nature of the human being follows, along with a discussion of dreams, sleep, death, life between death and rebirth, and reincarnation. In the fourth chapter evolution is described from the perspective of initiation science. The fifth chapter characterizes the training a student must undertake as a preparation for initiation. The sixth and seventh chapters consider the future evolution of the world and more detailed observations regarding supersensible realities.

(388 pp)	0-91014-275-0	Paper, $9.95 #113
	0-91014-226-2	Cloth, $16.00 #112

KNOWLEDGE OF THE HIGHER WORLDS AND ITS ATTAINMENT
by Rudolf Steiner

Rudolf Steiner's fundamental work on the path to higher knowledge explains in detail the exercises and disciplines a student must pursue in order to attain a wakeful experience of supersensible realities. The stages of Preparation, Enlightenment, and Initiation are described, as the transformation of dream life and the meeting with the Guardian of the Threshold. Moral exercises for developing each of the spiritual lotus petal organs ("chakras") are given in accordance with the rule of taking three steps in moral development for each step into spiritual knowledge. The path described here is a safe one which will not interfere with the student's ability to lead a normal outer life.

(237 pp)	0-88010-046-X	Paper, $6.95 #80
	0-88010-045-1	Cloth, $14.00 #363

ORDERING INFORMATION

All the books described on the preceding pages are available from:

Anthroposophic Press
Bell's Pond
Star Route
Hudson, NY 12534

Please send your payment with order (check or money order to Anthroposophic Press, Inc.). Add $1.75 for postage and handling. New York State residents please add sales tax which applies to your locality.

Free catalog listing hundreds of titles available on request.